AT HOME
KITC

AT HOME IN THE KITCHEN

Simple recipes from a chef's night off

David Kinch
with **Devin Fuller**

Photography by Aya Brackett

TEN SPEED PRESS
California | New York

This book is dedicated to all of those who've

passed through the doors at the Pink Palace.

Foreword

Having been a chef for most of my life, I've been privileged to meet many artists in my field. Very few are as inspiring as my friend David Kinch. David is that rare chef who combines warmth and artistry not only in his food, but also in how he walks in the world.

In 2009, I drove north to eat at Manresa. I had watched David's career from afar for many years and being able to finally meet him was a dream come true. It was a magical night and, by the end of it, I knew I had met a friend for life.

Soon after, I was invited to David's home for one of his regular dinner parties. I remember watching him joyfully prepare a truffled chicken, taking care to butter every inch and stop to smell the sweet fragrance of the truffles with his eyes closed and a smile on his face. His gorgeous table was bursting with color and flavor. His eggplant dip and homemade fava bean hummus, the oysters with their perfect vinaigrette, and the pure green salad reminded me of growing up in France. Everything he prepared was thoughtful, yet simple, using the finest ingredients all locally sourced.

As much as his food impressed me that evening—and on many evenings to follow—it was David's humanity and kindness that I was taken by. He showed me that one could be successful in our field while continuing to live by the values that we share: community, connection, and respect for nature and our craft.

Since that evening, David and I have had the honor of cooking together in Italy, San Francisco, and Los Angeles and sharing countless meals around the world. He is always a calm presence in a kitchen that can oftentimes be hectic. I've learned so much from him and am happy that the world will now get to cook with him by reading this book. Aside from the recipes, his adventurous spirit will take you on a journey to the places he has traveled that inspire him and through the music that feeds his soul.

In this book, you see the soul of a chef. You feel David's humanity and his unique ability to translate his love and care of food and people through his recipes. Simple, fresh produce take on extraordinary flavor in David's cooking. You've never tasted an avocado properly until you've tried his Guacamole with Pomegranate. The Orecchiette & Broccoli alla Romana is one of my favorites. He knows how to layer flavors but keep the integrity of the broccoli. In fact, he has a deep understanding of layering flavor in all of his dishes.

This new book is a celebration of who he is and how much he wants to break bread with you. Bon appétit!

—Dominique Crenn

Introduction

The year I started at Manresa was slated to be my worst. I left my boyfriend, spent two days packing whatever could fit into my tiny car, and drove 10 hours south to move back in with my parents at the age of 26. I started at the three-Michelin-star restaurant the next day as a polisher, which is exactly what it sounds like. I was thrown into one of the most intense environments I had ever known with one task: to polish every piece of glass and silver used during service. Buffing glasses and dishes was thankfully my only job, as it was all I was qualified for. I broke two stems on my first night, which, in fine dining, is more than your allotment for the entire year. I'll never forget when Chef Kinch (I'll call him David from now on for the sake of brevity, though it still makes me uncomfortable) looked at me with my hair falling out of place, disheveled, and brimming with anxiety, and said, "Don't be afraid to make mistakes."

About a month after that first day, I was invited by one of the sous chefs to attend a Tuesday sailing trip with David and the kitchen crew near Santa Cruz, a surf town on the California coast. I brought a cooler full of beer, an inexplicable bag of mandarins purchased in a panic at the register, and not enough warm clothes. We spent hours on the Pacific Ocean, shoveling spicy snapper ceviche onto Juanita's tortilla chips and washing down homemade pastrami on rye with deli mustard and half-sour pickles with Pacifico and lime. I felt the beginnings of a door opening, a glimpse into a world where the utmost pleasures in life come from sharing time, food, and drinks with the people you love.

As I moved up the ranks at Manresa, my memory is marked in epochs by occasions like these. Many nights were spent at David's pink house down the street. A start-of-summer paella party. A wild, twelve-hour holiday dinner party—playing limbo with an old broom handle and dancing to Donna Summer's "I Feel Love" until four in the morning. One of the best pastas of my life, thrown together with cans from the pantry after a staff bowling party. Roast chickens. Too many oysters to count.

David went from being an elusive chef to a dear friend over my years at Manresa, our friendship sparked by a shared love of chess, rhum, music, and, naturally, food and its unmatched power to bring people together. He has become a mentor and confidant. We have celebrated successes and supported each other through hardships.

When he approached me about writing this book together, I was both humbled and honored. I have been in the unique position to learn the delights of the dining table from a top-ten chef first-hand. But more than that, I've gotten to know the man behind the curtain. I'm proud to introduce you to him, so he might enrich your life in some of the ways he has enriched mine.

Heartbreak, a move, a career change: through these clichéd yet traumatic coming-of-age moments, I was extremely lucky. I had a place to stay. I had the opportunity to work at one of the world's best restaurants. I had a once-in-a-lifetime chance to meet David Kinch, who has spent more than forty years in kitchens, has been named one of the best chefs in the world, and still spends his weekends making food for friends simply because it brings him joy.

David has dedicated his life to curiosity, continuous learning, tireless ambition, and having a damn good time in the process. In this book, you'll have the opportunity to meet David, too. You'll learn from him, cook with him, share a drink with him. He'll show you the simple recipes he genuinely enjoys making on his days off. He'll help you throw a spectacular party, or just throw something together when you're hungry after a long night.

And, best of all, he'll give you room to make mistakes.

—Devin Fuller

I took my first kitchen job—at the Commander's Palace—when I was 16, not because I wanted to be in the restaurant industry, but because I wanted to cook. Forty years later, I still want to cook. Manresa is one expression of my love for cooking. But another expression, more intimate in many ways, are my Tuesday nights. As a working chef, my days off are Monday and Tuesday: that's my weekend. Tuesdays are my Sundays. On Tuesdays, I'm at my most comfortable. That's my time to cook at home for those I love. On Tuesdays, I make my comfort foods. I play. On Tuesdays, I cook for me.

For the better part of my adult life, my working days have been spent running kitchens. It's been many years since my first shift as a line cook, and I still choose to spend my days off making food for myself and my friends and family at the "Pink Palace"—a nickname affectionately bestowed by my friends on my strawberry-colored home in Santa Cruz, California. More often than not, I spend my Tuesdays on my front porch with a glass of wine in hand, vinyl playing on the turntable, and something simple cooking on the stove.

In this book, I welcome you to the Pink Palace on my day off: to my home on a Tuesday. I wrote it because of a natural desire to share all the special memories I've made cooking at home. But more so, I wanted to impart some of the knowledge I've acquired after so many years in professional kitchens.

I've kept each recipe simple, with only a handful of ingredients that I find at my local market. I did this not because I don't think you're capable of more, but because these are the dishes I genuinely love to make. When people ask me what I like to cook most, the answer is always the same: roast chicken. I swear to you, I learn something new every time I roast a chicken. Cooking has given me not only a career and a purpose, but it's also given me endless opportunities to learn. I truly believe that learning is one of the greatest pleasures of life. I hope you'll learn something from this book—maybe a practical skill, a go-to weeknight salmon dish, or an omelet to share on a lazy Sunday.

The truth is that I don't think cooking is difficult. I do, however, think it requires attention. Just like anything else worth doing, it's worth doing well. I say this not only in terms of technique—after all, there's a right way to poach an egg and I'll share it with you—but also with regard to the emotional reverence required for cooking. You don't need a professional kitchen or a culinary degree to use this book; all I ask for is your attention. I don't do so with frivolity: when I ask you to learn something new, it will be worth your time. Because, in the end, knowing how to shuck an oyster

will make you a finer host. Knowing how to prepare a risotto will make you a better date. And knowing how to make a grilled cheese sandwich will make you a happier person at two o'clock in the morning.

I had a lot of fun writing this cookbook, reflecting on the memories of each dish and all the kitchen has given me throughout my life. When I consider my future, I imagine moving to an island somewhere, swimming in the ocean every day, wearing a shirt infrequently, and cooking dinner at home every night. Until then, I have my Tuesdays.

On Tuesdays, I spend my days by the beach. Sometimes I surf, sometimes I pack a book and drive my scooter to the water, then stop by the gelato shop or the wine store on my way home. I rinse off the sand, lie down on my living room floor, and listen to my favorite records. You'll notice that each recipe includes a song suggestion from my collection. I spent the bulk of my formative years in New Orleans—not only in kitchens, but also immersing myself in the city's vibrant music scene. This playlist is my opportunity to take care of something for you. I can't come to your house to make the pesto, but I can tell you to chill your mortar and pestle and listen to Aretha Franklin's best song while you do it. I like to imagine that you've thought of every detail for your evening except the music, and my playlist comes through for you at the last second. But really, I did this part of the book for myself, just for fun. Either way, I hope you find a couple of songs that put you on your living room floor, too.

I'm surrounded by a wonderful team at my restaurants. They support me and inspire me. But, these days I spend service directing the kitchen, not standing behind the stoves. On Tuesdays, I chop the onions. I fix the sauce that I've left simmering for too long while I play with Ella, my cat. On Tuesdays, I don't have my professional kitchen. I'm not using fancy equipment or ingredients; I shop for products down the street. On Tuesdays, I just cook for fun. Welcome to my Tuesday.

—David Kinch

It Helps to Know

For the purposes of this cookbook . . .

Here are answers to the questions you would ask your chef friend, and other practical advice for using this book.

Basil loses a lot of its aroma when washed, so I recommend you use the highest-quality unwashed organic basil you can find. If that's not an option, clean your basil gently using a damp paper towel.

All butter is unsalted.

All cheese is fresh and freshly grated. I typically grate cheese on the large side of a box grater. There are some cases where I call for "cheese, finely grated." For this, I use a Microplane grater, an inexpensive kitchen tool I highly recommend.

Any wine called for in a recipe is always dry unless otherwise specified. I prefer using wine with no discernible oak. Sauvignon Blanc, Pinot Bianco, and most Italian whites work well. Avoid Chardonnay because it tends to be over-oaked, which tastes bitter when reduced. You don't need to spend a fortune but it should taste good. I recommend getting a bottle you actually want to drink, and using some of it for the food.

Crack eggs on the counter (not on the edge of a bowl) to avoid driving broken eggshell into the egg. Also, all eggs are assumed large.

Extra-virgin olive oil should be mild and buttery, not peppery or bold.

If your garlic clove has a green germ in the center, remove and discard it; it's bitter.

It's difficult to maneuver around the knots and odd shapes of ginger with a vegetable peeler. Scrape it with the edge of a metal spoon.

Salt is kosher unless otherwise specified. For some recipes I've called for flaky sea salt, which is the large finishing salt you can find at your grocery store. There are plenty of solid options; I use Maldon, Jacobsen, or sel de Guérande.

I don't use a food processor to chop vegetables. Machines pulverize: they shatter and crush the vegetable instead of cutting it. Take the time to cut things by hand—your food will taste better. "Diced" vegetables should be cut to the exact same size and shape, which makes the finished dish especially pretty. "Chopped" vegetables should also be cut to the same size so they cook evenly, but they don't need to be perfect. "Minced" vegetables should simply be cut to a very small dice.

I salt my water after it's boiling, as doing so before may stain the bottom of your pot. And speaking of salting water . . . I use a lot of salt in my pasta water. When you taste it, it should remind you of the ocean.

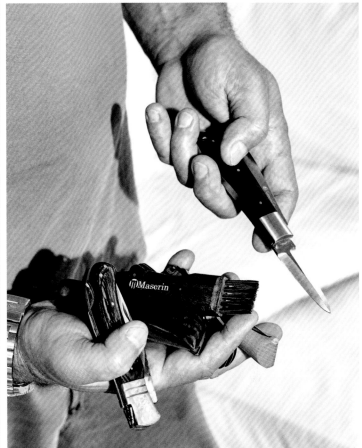

BIG
JOHN COLTRANE
SUPER SAVER SERIES
THE KINK
CL 644
MAHALIA
Miles Davis
In A Silent Way
STEREO
THE FABULOUS
JOHNNY CASH
COLUMBIA
LUSH LIFE / JOHN COLTRANE
ROLLING STONES LET IT BLEED
KINK

Butter the Size of a Walnut

My first memories in the kitchen come from watching my grandmothers cook for our weekly family gathering. I'd observe as they prepared long-simmered meats, or rivels (Pennsylvania Dutch dumplings) and beans, or a chicken and corn pie straight out of the oven with a glass of warm milk poured over the top. Aside from specific dishes, there's one detail of my grandmothers' cooking that's stuck with me all these years. It's a commonality I've found in some of the most austere French cookbooks I've studied as a chef, and it was on my mind nearly every day I spent developing the recipes for this book: ingredients and their measures were often described in visual terms, like "butter the size of a walnut" or "half a glass of white wine."

In writing this book, I was tasked with detailing how I cook in concrete amounts. Devin was constantly asking, "How long did it take to brown the onions?" or, "How many tablespoons of oil was that?" My response was often acerbic, "I cooked them until they were brown," or, "I added oil until it was coated." We'd go back and forth until I conceded and gave her an estimate.

What I value most about my time learning from my grandmothers is that a directive like "the size of a walnut" forced me to cook with my eyes. I wasn't measuring an exact tablespoon or setting a timer as soon as I put the onions in the pan. Instead, I watched the onions until they turned golden, or until they were barely softened, depending on what was called for. This gave me confidence in my cooking—not because I was talented, but rather because I learned that cooking for myself, family, and friends has a relatively low margin of error.

When it comes to using this book, everything is an estimate—albeit a thoughtful one. A potato will roast differently depending on how thinly you sliced it and how hot 400°F actually is in your oven. So, if I say about 30 minutes, and the potatoes crunch when you take a bite, put the pan back in your oven and keep checking until they're cooked through. Learn to let the onions sit until they're a little softer, even if I said about 7 minutes and it's been 8½. Maybe they'll start to turn brown and the next time you'll take them off a minute sooner. I give estimates for cook times (mostly because a harmonious life is about compromise), but, like my grandmothers' instructions, these recipes are intended to be made with your eyes. This asks you to pay attention, but I believe it's worth the extra effort.

If I had to describe the philosophy of this book, I would say that it's more intangible than just passing along simple recipes that I've collected and loved over the years. In my perfect world, you'll use this book to make and savor my favorite dishes, but also learn life skills that will help you have fun in the kitchen—just as I did while I learned to watch a walnut-size pat of butter melt in my grandmother's pan until it turned foamy and brown, and we cooked the onions for a few minutes too long.

SMALL PLATES TO COVER YOUR TABLE + CONDIMENTS TO FILL YOUR PANTRY

1

I don't have a formal dining room. Walking up to my porch on a summer evening, you would be likely to pass by a few friends sitting on the stoop, drinking chilled wine and watching the sunset. Through the front door, you'll find my living room filled with records, photography books, Stones memorabilia, instruments, bicycles, art, and various items of nostalgia that make me feel at home. In the corner, surrounded by bay windows, sits a circular table that's rarely used for dining as it's almost always covered by a jigsaw puzzle.

Moving through the living room brings you to what best passes as my dining table, nestled between tall windows and my kitchen island. It's a relatively small teak table with four chairs that's usually hidden beneath cookbooks and yellow notepads scribbled with recipes and ideas.

When I'm having friends over, I put away my work, extend the table's leaves on both sides, and cover its surface with food. Dips, spreads, salads, and mezzes fill every square inch—a handful of my favorite small plates collected from years working in restaurants around the world. Filling up my table in this way gives guests an idea of what to expect. Instead of a lonely bowl of chips and salsa, for example, an abundance awaits them the second they walk in the door. The tone is set: one of festive, yet modest extravagance. Guests relax before their first drink, anticipating the evening to come.

This kind of presentation doesn't take a week's worth of preparation, nor does it require a huge budget. The recipes in this chapter are quick and inexpensive enough to make a handful for a party, or to prepare for yourself as snacks during the week. What makes them special is their simplicity: each recipe highlights a few fresh ingredients in the best way I know how.

I've also included in this chapter some key pantry ingredients that I always keep on hand: stocks to prepare in advance, like chickpea (see page 34) and Parmesan (see page 33), as well as sides, like my roast shallots (see page 31) and pickles (see page 28), which will give you a chance to get creative with flavor.

These recipes are the product of years spent traveling: eating on porches, around a table, or on the street. I wrote them from memory; I have made every one of these hundreds of times. They celebrate the small things and simple ingredients that bring me joy. Whether you're making them for yourself, or to fill your pantry, or to cover your dining table, I hope they help you celebrate the small things, too.

Mother-Sauce Mayo

Makes about 1¼ cups

1 egg yolk, at room temperature

1 tablespoon white wine vinegar

Scant cup sunflower oil

Salt

Dijon mustard, freshly squeezed lemon juice, or sriracha, for seasoning (optional)

Everyone's quick to praise aioli, but they're less willing to profess their love for its more understated cousin: mayonnaise. I, on the other hand, describe mayonnaise as "the home" because you can season it to your liking and put it on just about anything. It's hard to believe that nearly a cup of oil can be emulsified into one egg yolk, but I assure you that, with some patience, a room-temperature egg can turn into what I consider to be the ultimate mother sauce. It takes a little more effort, yes, but a homemade, hand-whisked mayo makes all the difference in the world.

Place the yolk in a large bowl and add the vinegar. Using a hand whisk, whisk until combined. Continue to vigorously whisk the yolk while you add the oil in very small increments. (And when I say small, I mean three drops at a time, especially to start. If you accidentally add too much oil at once, the sauce will break. In this case, your best option is to start over.)

Continue to add the oil and whisk as the sauce starts to thicken. When it becomes very thick and difficult to whisk, add a small splash of cold water and a pinch of salt. Continue with this process patiently, until you've whisked in all of the oil. Continue to add water when you notice the mayonnaise becoming too thick.

Season with a few large pinches of salt, adding more to taste. With most things, and especially with mayonnaise, it's important to get the salt level correct before you add other seasonings. Whisk in the additional seasonings as desired and adjust to your liking.

Use immediately, or store covered in your refrigerator for up to 4 days.

Pairs well with "Let's Stick Together" by Wilbert Harrison

Mignonette

Makes about ½ cup

1 teaspoon black peppercorns

1 medium shallot, finely diced

½ cup red or white wine vinegar
   (I prefer white)

This is a straightforward mignonette—with one small upgrade: I let the aromatics marinate and then strain the liquid to avoid chewing on peppercorns. Serve alongside plenty of fresh oysters (see page 21).

Coarsely crush the peppercorns using a mortar and pestle. If you don't have a mortar and pestle, set the peppercorns on a sturdy cutting board, and, using the bottom edge of a pot, firmly press down and forward on the peppercorns until each one is crushed. Don't be afraid to be aggressive. Both methods will yield peppercorns of all different sizes, and that's what you want.

Combine the peppercorns, half the shallots, and the vinegar in a bowl, stir, and let sit for 30 minutes.

Pour the mixture through a fine-mesh strainer set over a bowl, reserving the vinegar and discarding the peppercorns and shallots. Add the remaining shallots, stir, and serve.

Pairs well with *"Garbageman" by The Cramps*

How to Shuck an Oyster

I have a few rules about oysters. I only eat them during months spelled with the letter R (a helpful trick for remembering when they're in season). I don't order six oysters to share. On the conservative side, nine oysters per person is an acceptable portion—a number I picked up from a Parisian bar owner who told me from three tables down that I'd been eating oysters incorrectly my entire life. I've eaten the muscle ever since. Most importantly, I always take the oyster knife away from any friend who looks like they're about to take off their hand.

- To prepare, rinse off any sand and dirt from the oyster's shell using cold water. Fill your serving bowl with ice. I prefer crushed ice so I can force the oyster to lie flat, but any ice you have on hand will do.

- Fold a thick cloth towel in half. Don't use your nice linen; this towel's about to get very dirty.

- Notice the oyster's shape: an oval with one rounded end and one end that tapers to a point. There's a deep convex bottom shell and a flat top shell.

- Set the oyster on the folded towel with the flat shell facing up and the tapered end pointing toward your dominant hand.

- Fold the towel over the rounded end so the tapered end is exposed. Use your nondominant hand to hold the oyster in place, with your hand pressing into the towel to prevent the oyster from slipping.

- Wiggle the knife into the tapered end of the oyster, twisting your hand to find the hinge. Be sure to point the knife downward and keep your steadying hand at a distance in case you accidentally slip.

- Twist the knife like you're turning a key in a lock until you feel the shell release.

- Before opening the oyster, run the shucker along the inside of the top flat shell to separate the muscle. This requires some finesse: be careful to cut only the muscle and not the oyster itself.

- You should be left with the bottom shell containing the intact oyster and its liquid. Wipe off your shucker and carefully separate the muscle from the bottom shell in a scooping motion.

- Smell the oyster. If you smell rotten fish, toss it. If you smell fresh brine that transports you to a sailboat in the middle of the ocean, shove it in the ice and serve it immediately, alongside the mignonette.

Seven-Ingredient Pesto, Two Ways

Makes ¾ cup (enough for a lot of
pasta as a little pesto goes a long way)

I have a lot of opinions when it comes to pesto, mostly because it's one of a select handful of things I consider sacred. Rest assured that I don't say this lightly: I believe it's the single greatest sauce in Italian cuisine.

The Right Way

½ cup finely grated Parmigiano-
Reggiano

½ cup finely grated Pecorino Romano

1 clove garlic

Flaky sea salt

3 tablespoons pine nuts

2 cups lightly packed basil leaves
(young and tender preferred)

¼ to ½ cup extra-virgin olive oil

**It helps to know: This recipe
requires a cold mortar and
pestle (I use a marble mortar
and a wooden pestle, but
inexpensive options are
abundant on the internet).
I use unwashed basil leaves
to maintain their aroma.
If your basil is dirty, clean
it carefully using a damp
paper towel.**

I kept things simple whenever possible for this book because I want you to feel you can not only tackle, but also enjoy cooking these recipes. Pesto is one of the few cases where I will adamantly urge you to make it the "low-tech" way. The result is delicate and vibrant, and in the time it takes to boil water for pasta, you'll have used your hands to create something truly special.

Cool your mortar and pestle in your refrigerator for at least 30 minutes. (The two worst things you can do to pesto are to overheat it and use too much.)

In a small bowl, stir together the cheeses, and set aside.

Place a folded towel beneath the cold mortar to allow it to rotate more easily. Using the pestle, mash the garlic with a pinch of salt to form a paste. Add the pine nuts and begin stirring the pestle aggressively around the center to force the ingredients up the sides of the mortar. Turn the bowl as you pound the pestle down along the sides.

When the pine nuts and garlic have formed a paste, begin adding the basil in small handfuls, adding a pinch of salt occasionally to act as an abrasive. Continue to stir the ingredients up the sides of the mortar, rotate the bowl, and hit the pestle along its sides. With a little patience, gravity will do the work for you. Continue with this process until you've added all of the basil and no large leaves remain. The leaves will be a variety of sizes—imperfection is part of the beauty of a handmade pesto.

Add the cheese mixture in small spoonfuls, continuing to stir, rotate, and pound the ingredients together.

Slowly add the olive oil, still stirring and pounding until the pesto transforms from a paste to a thick, creamy sauce with a little flow. The amount of olive oil you use will vary depending on your preference, but ¼ to ½ cup usually does the trick. Be careful not to add too much oil too quickly as it will separate.

Use immediately, or store in your refrigerator covered in ½ inch olive oil for up to 6 months. The olive oil preserves the pesto by preventing any contact with air. When you're ready to serve, simply remove the excess oil and give the pesto a good stir.

The Other Way

1 clove garlic

3 tablespoons pine nuts

Flaky sea salt

2 cups lightly packed basil leaves and stems

½ cup finely grated Parmigiano-Reggiano

½ cup finely grated Pecorino Romano

¼ to ½ cup extra-virgin olive oil

It helps to know: **This recipe requires a food processor or blender.**

Before opening my new restaurant, Mentone, I traveled to Italy to learn the classic techniques of Genovese cuisine. On one of my trips, Roberto Panizza (the godfather of pesto) recounted the heartbreak of watching his grandmother prepare pesto using a blender. Use the following recipe if you must, but know that you'll break Mr. Panizza's (and my) heart.

Pulse the garlic, pine nuts, and a pinch of salt in a food processor until a paste forms. Add the basil and pulse until smooth.

Add the cheeses, turn the machine to low, and drizzle in the olive oil until the pesto transforms from a paste to a sauce.

Use immediately, or store in your refrigerator covered with ½ inch olive oil for up to 6 months.

Pairs well with *"Dr. Feelgood (Love Is a Serious Business)" by Aretha Franklin*

How to Dress a Salad

When making a salad with delicate leafy greens, I usually don't make a dressing. The two things I want to taste in a simple green salad are the lettuce and the olive oil. I start by adding a very small amount of olive oil to the greens—just enough so they're barely coated. Then I add a touch of vinegar or lemon juice. Always err on the side of too little vinegar rather than too much. I like the lettuce to be the predominant taste, and the acidity to be more of a nuance.

For heartier greens or a more composed salad, I whisk the dressing in a bowl and pour it over the top, maintaining the less-is-more philosophy. As much as I love to spoon juices over finished dishes, in this case, your empty salad plate should be left with a faint shimmer of oil and nothing more. The greens should be barely coated, not heavy or wet. And as with most things, I season with salt (and sometimes pepper) to taste.

For any of the following vinaigrettes, it is perfectly acceptable (and delicious!) to substitute half of the olive oil with a high-quality walnut oil.

A Few Standard Vinaigrettes

SIMPLE Makes about ½ cup

In a small bowl, dissolve a pinch of salt in the juice of ½ lemon. Whisk in a scant ½ cup of your best olive oil.

CLASSIC Makes about 1¼ cups

In a small bowl, combine 1 diced shallot with ¼ cup aromatic vinegar (I like red wine or sherry). Set aside for 15 minutes to mellow out the flavor of the shallot. Dissolve a pinch of salt in the vinegar, then whisk in a scant 1 cup of your best olive oil and a few turns from a pepper mill.

MUSTARDY Makes about 1¼ cups

Make the Classic (above), and add ½ teaspoon Dijon mustard to the vinegar. Keep in mind: a little bit of mustard goes a long way.

LEMONY Makes about ⅓ cup

In a small bowl, mix together a pinch of salt, ½ teaspoon Dijon mustard, and the juice of ½ lemon. Whisk in ¼ cup of your best olive oil and the zest from 1 lemon. Let the dressing marinate for about 15 minutes before using.

Garlicky Herbed Croutons

Makes about 3 cups

3 tablespoons butter

3 tablespoons extra-virgin olive oil

2 cloves garlic, smashed and finely chopped

1 tablespoon fresh thyme leaves, coarsely chopped

½ teaspoon fresh rosemary leaves, coarsely chopped

1 pound levain bread, crust discarded and middle torn into bite-size pieces

Salt and freshly ground black pepper

These croutons are crunchy on the outside and soft on the inside—ideal for salads or on top of soup. I like to tear the bread by hand to make interesting shapes, and I don't make them overly crispy: if you want a super crispy, perfectly square crouton you might as well buy them at the store. You'll likely end up with too many croutons for a salad, but you'll want to snack on half of them anyway.

Preheat your oven to 400°F. Line a large baking sheet with aluminum foil.

In a small pot on low heat, mix together the butter and olive oil. When the butter has melted and combined with the oil, add the garlic and herbs and stir until fragrant, about 1 minute.

In a large bowl, pour the olive oil mixture over the torn bread. Top with two healthy pinches each of salt and pepper and stir to combine. Set aside to allow the bread to absorb the oil, stirring occasionally until you no longer see a pool at the bottom of the bowl, about 4 minutes.

Spread the bread in a single layer on the baking sheet (it's okay for the bread to touch, just make sure it's in one single layer).

Bake, tossing occasionally, until the croutons are crispy and have turned a dark brown around the edges, about 15 minutes. Set aside to cool to room temperature.

Use immediately, or store in an airtight container in your refrigerator for up to 1 day.

Pairs well with *"Soul Sister" by Allen Toussaint*

A Quick Pickle, Japanese Style

Yield is variable

PICKLING LIQUID

Water

Dry white wine

Rice vinegar

Sugar

Salt

COLD PICKLE IDEAS

Melon, cubed, with mint leaves

Onions, sliced

Peaches, sliced, with basil leaves

Plums, quartered

HOT PICKLE IDEAS

Beets, roasted and cubed

Carrots, sliced, with whole jalapeños

Cucumbers, whole

Eggplant, blanched and cubed

Turnips, blanched

Zucchini, cubed

Pickles are an easy way to add acidity to a dish, especially raw fish or salads, or to serve as a side to roasted meat. This very light pickle base is a flavoring pickle; it's not intended to preserve the fruit or vegetable but rather to add a sweet-and-sour punch. This is my go-to pickle base because it pickles both fruits and vegetables without overpowering their flavor or causing them to lose their natural crunch. The pickle base is made from equal parts (by volume) water, white wine, rice vinegar, and sugar. The amount of liquid you need depends on the amount of produce you're pickling. Get creative with what you pickle! Make a big batch and store it in your refrigerator for a simple way to elevate your meals throughout the week.

In a small pot on high heat, add equal amounts of water, wine, vinegar, and sugar and stir to combine. (Be sure the liquid will fully cover your chosen mixture of vegetables, fruits, and herbs when it's poured into the pickling container.) Bring the liquid to a simmer, stirring frequently, until the sugar dissolves. Add salt to taste.

From here, you can go one of two ways. If you're pickling a soft fruit or vegetable, let your pickling liquid cool to room temperature before pouring it over the top. If you're pickling a tougher vegetable, pour the liquid directly over the fruits or vegetables while it's still hot.

Put your chosen vegetables, fruits, and a handful of herbs into a jar and pour in the pickling liquid. Cover the jar and put it in your refrigerator to pickle for at least 24 hours or up to 2 weeks.

Pairs well with "Get Down" by Curtis Mayfield

Roast Shallots in Space

Yield is variable

Large shallots (as many as you'd like)
Salt
Extra-virgin olive oil

With this method, the shallots are suspended on an aluminum-foil bed while they cook—essentially floating in space while they roast without touching the hot pan. This makes supple, sweet shallots that fully soften without burning: an incredible accompaniment to roasted meat, such as Roast Chicken (page 202) or Pork Tenderloins with Coriander & Fennel (page 186). Though best served fresh, the shallots will keep in an airtight container in your refrigerator for up to 2 days. Note that they may lose some of their eat-on-their-own-worthy flavor and texture with age. If you find yourself with leftovers, treat them like an extra-sweet fresh onion and spread them on a sandwich or chop and whisk them into a vinaigrette (see page 24) or Mother-Sauce Mayo (page 17).

Preheat your oven to 425°F.

Trim off the bottom of the shallots. Discard the papery peel that easily falls off, leaving the thin layer or two of peel that remains stuck to the bulb. Cut off the tops and set the shallots in a large bowl. Add a pinch of salt, drizzle with oil, and toss until coated.

Line an ovenproof pan or baking dish with aluminum foil, pushing the foil up around the sides of the pan and along its rim. Repeat with one more piece of foil, so the pan is double-lined. Don't push too hard between the two layers—you want to allow for some air pockets so the shallots "float" as they bake.

Spread the shallots evenly in the pan and cover it again with aluminum foil, pushing on the outer edge to create a seal. Roast for 35 minutes, shaking occasionally to toss.

Remove the shallots from your oven, remove the top layer of foil, and set aside to cool in the pan.

Once the shallots have cooled to room temperature, set each one flat on its cut side and squeeze to force it out of its skin. I serve them halfway out of their skins because I like the way it looks, but you can also discard the skin entirely.

Pairs well with "Blues Walk" by Lou Donaldson

Chicken Stock

Makes about 8 cups

Leftover bones and meat from
   1 Roast Chicken (page 202)

1 white or yellow onion, quartered

1 rib celery, chopped

1 carrot, peeled (or thoroughly
   washed) and chopped

1 bay leaf

5 sprigs flat-leaf parsley

This basic chicken stock isn't intended to be groundbreaking, but rather a "Why not make it?" when you roast a chicken. Homemade stock is always better than store-bought not only for its flavor, but also because you can add salt later as you please. Plus, making chicken stock is incredibly easy (you can make it while you eat the chicken!). Use this stock in almost any recipe in place of water, including Chickpea Minestrone, Genovese Style (page 214), Onion & Brioche Soup with a Poached Egg & Manchego (page 92), or Jambalaya, New Orleans Style (page 152), or even to add flavor to cooked rice. Alternatively, you can store it in an airtight container in the freezer for up to 3 months. Like I said, why not?

In a large pot on high heat, combine the chicken leftovers, onion, celery, carrot, bay leaf, and parsley and add cold water to cover. When a foamy scum forms on top of the water, skim it off and discard.

Turn the heat to low to maintain a gentle simmer and cover the pot with the lid slightly ajar to allow steam to escape. Let simmer for 2 hours.

Strain over a large bowl and use immediately, or store the stock in an airtight container in the freezer for up to 3 months.

Pairs well with "Love My Baby" by Hayden Thompson

Parmesan Stock

Makes about 8 cups

8 ounces Parmigiano-Reggiano rinds, large pieces broken up

I use this stock in place of water for adding a umami-rich Parmesan flavor to so many dishes, especially white beans, risotto, tomato soup, and rice. It can be made with fresh Parmigiano-Reggiano, but that would be a waste of expensive cheese. Start saving the end pieces that get grated to death and then thrown away. Tightly wrap them in plastic and save in the freezer until you have 8 ounces of rinds (or make friends with your local cheesemonger).

In a medium pot on high heat, bring the rinds (frozen is okay) and 10 cups water to a boil. Once boiling, turn the heat to low and cover the pot with the lid slightly ajar to allow steam to escape. Let simmer for 1½ hours.

Remove the pot from the heat and let it cool to room temperature. Strain over a large bowl, discarding the rinds. Use immediately or store the stock in an airtight container in the freezer for up to 3 months.

Pairs well with "What Do I Get?" by Buzzcocks

Chickpea Stock

Makes about 8 cups stock and
4 cups chickpeas

2 cups dried chickpeas

1 bay leaf

2 pieces star anise

4 sprigs thyme

1 head garlic, bottom root trimmed,
  head halved horizontally, skin on

1 teaspoon black peppercorns

1 medium white onion, halved

2 carrots, ends discarded and peeled

1 teaspoon sugar

Salt

If you find yourself wondering why soups and sauces at restaurants taste so much better than the ones you make at home, it's probably because restaurants use house-made stock. Stock is the foundation of a dish, and particularly good stock can be the jumping-off point that takes a home-cooked meal to the next level. This is a wonderful, versatile stock that happens to be vegetarian. Perfect for Date-Night Risotto with Crab (page 147) or Chickpea Minestrone, Genovese Style (page 214), this stock, in particular, can also be widely used in place of water for just about any recipe to add complexity of flavor. This recipe also leaves you with 4 cups of cooked chickpeas. I recommend using them for the Raw Fava, Chickpea & Tahini Hummus (opposite).

In a large pot, immerse the chickpeas in water and soak for 2 hours. Alternatively, you can soak overnight, but decrease the cook time to around 1 hour in total so as not to overcook the chickpeas.

Drain the chickpeas and discard the water. Wrap the bay leaf, star anise, thyme, garlic, and peppercorns in cheesecloth and tie shut with string to make a sachet.

In a large pot on high heat, bring the chickpeas and 10 cups water to a simmer. The pot will form a scum resembling soap suds. Skim off the scum and turn the heat to low. Add the onion, carrots, herb sachet, and sugar and bring the stock back to a simmer.

After 45 minutes, stir in a couple pinches of salt. Avoid the temptation to add salt at the beginning because this toughens the skin of the chickpeas. Continue to simmer, uncovered, until the chickpeas have cooked through, about 45 minutes more. The chickpeas are finished when they no longer taste dry but still retain some of their texture.

Remove the pot from the heat, cover, and let the chickpeas cool completely in their broth, ideally overnight. This allows the final extraction of flavor, and the result will merit the extra time.

Remove the herb sachet, carrots, and onions and discard. Strain the chickpeas over a large bowl to reserve the stock. Both the stock and the chickpeas can be used immediately or stored separately in airtight containers in the freezer for up to 3 months.

It helps to know: **This stock sits overnight and requires cheesecloth.**

Pairs well with "Cadillac Lane" by Buck Owens

Raw Fava, Chickpea & Tahini Hummus

Serves 4 to 6

1 cup raw fava beans

1 cup cooked or canned chickpeas

1 clove garlic

½ cup tahini

¾ cup extra-virgin olive oil, plus
more for drizzling

1 teaspoon salt

Juice of 1 Meyer lemon

1 teaspoon za'atar for garnish

Handful of fresh mint leaves for
garnish (optional)

**It helps to know: This recipe
requires a food processor
or blender.**

Yes, you can easily buy hummus at the grocery store, but this fava and tahini spread (see photo, pages 50–51) puts store-bought hummus to shame. The fresh, raw favas taste like springtime, and combined with the creamy, nutty tahini, you'll find yourself eating it directly from a spoon. Serve alongside raw vegetables and pita chips at a dinner party, on crusty toast for breakfast, or as a spread for sandwiches throughout the week. Use the cooked chickpeas from Chickpea Stock (opposite), or canned chickpeas in a pinch.

Blanch the beans by dunking them in boiling water for 30 seconds. Drain and run cold water over them to stop the cooking process. Pop the beans out of their pod and use a small knife to peel and discard the outer skin.

Add the peeled favas, chickpeas, and garlic to a food processor and pulse until combined. With the food processor on low speed, add the tahini. Once combined, drizzle in the olive oil and mix to your desired consistency.

Transfer the mixture to a bowl, add the salt and lemon juice, and stir to combine.

Drizzle a healthy amount of olive oil over the top. Sprinkle with the za'atar and garnish with the mint leaves. Serve immediately, or smooth out the top and cover the hummus with olive oil. Store, covered in your refrigerator, for up to 1 week.

Pairs well with "I Can't Let Go" by Evie Sands

Everyone's a Pepperhead

An old chef friend of mine (who will remain nameless, as will the restaurant where this took place) told me an endearing story of when he first started working in kitchens as a young cook. And, since he told me with a massive grin on his face, I feel okay about sharing it with you.

He was from Brooklyn—well before it was the land of avocado toast—and he had never seen an avocado. He was handed a box of the fruit during prep and told to make a puree. Not wanting to expose his inexperience, he awkwardly peeled the avocados and put them into a blender whole, unaware that they had pits. Call it his lack of knowledge or call it bone-headedness, but what happened next earned him the title of "Pepperhead."

In this kitchen, pepperhead was a name reserved for those who did something of a dubious nature, like trying to puree avocados with their pits still inside. Another cook would cut off the top of a bell pepper with its stem intact, punch two holes in its sides, and string some butcher's twine through the holes to make a hat. For the rest of service that day, you had to wear the pepper hat; hence, you were a "pepperhead." The upside is that this happened in an influential restaurant, and my friend went on to have a very successful career. But, for a night, he was a pepperhead.

At some point as cooks, we will all undoubtedly and inevitably be pepperheads. Even the most established chefs have made wild mistakes in the kitchen, mistakes that would make the average home cook cringe. The truth is that mistakes shouldn't be avoided: they're part of learning, which is one of life's greatest gifts. If nothing else, they give us all an opportunity to laugh at ourselves. When you mess up, learn something new and keep cooking. To this day, when I roast a red bell pepper, I often think of my friend—the pepperhead—who stuck with it through all the mistakes until he became a chef.

Roasted Red Pepper & Onion Salad
with Mozzarella & Basil

Serves 6

2 large unpeeled white onions

Extra-virgin olive oil

Salt

4 large red bell peppers

12 ounces fresh mozzarella, cut into
   ½-inch rounds

Juice of 1 lemon

Freshly ground black pepper

2 tablespoons red wine vinegar

1 clove garlic, finely chopped

1 cup tightly packed small basil leaves
   (or large leaves cut with kitchen
   scissors)

**It helps to know: This recipe
requires a gas stove. See the
Red Pepper & Basil Relish
on page 41 for an alternative
roasting method.**

This salad is a standard on my table because it's objectively tasty, of course, but also because most of the preparation is simply allowing the ingredients to rest. The sweetness of the onions paired with the smokiness of the bell peppers is an easy sell, but what really shines has nothing to do with my cooking. I'm talking about one of my favorite things: plain mozzarella. Or, as I like to call it, "solid milk."

Preheat your oven to 400°F.

Coat the onions with olive oil, sprinkle with a pinch of salt, and wrap them tightly in aluminum foil. Roast on a baking sheet for 45 minutes. Set aside to cool to room temperature.

Meanwhile, with your gas burner on high, set one of the bell peppers directly on the grate. Allow the outer skin to char thoroughly on each side, using tongs to rotate until the entire pepper is black, 10 to 15 minutes. Roast one pepper at a time, or use all four burners to keep things extra exciting. You'll want your fan on and the windows open either way.

Set the blackened peppers in a large bowl and cover with plastic wrap, then set aside to cool to room temperature.

Spread the mozzarella on a large serving platter with space between each slice. Add a squeeze of lemon juice, a drizzle of olive oil, and a pinch each of salt and pepper. Set aside.

When the onions have cooled, remove them from the foil, reserving the pool of roasting liquid that's formed at the bottom. Peel and cut them into quarters. Place them in a large bowl along with their roasting liquid, allowing the wedges to fall apart into individual slices.

When the peppers have cooled, use your hands to peel off their skin. Remove the stem, rip them in half, and discard their seeds. Rinse with cold water and pat dry. Cut the peeled peppers into 1-inch-wide strips and mix them in with the onions, ½ cup olive oil, the vinegar, garlic, basil, and a pinch of salt.

Arrange the bell pepper and onion mixture around the mozzarella. Serve immediately.

Pairs well with "Town without Pity" by Gene Pitney

Red Pepper & Basil Relish

6 red bell peppers

¾ cup plus 2 tablespoons
extra-virgin olive oil

5 cloves garlic, thinly sliced

Salt

2 tablespoons sherry vinegar

8 small basil leaves (or large leaves
cut with kitchen scissors)

In this dish, I roast the red peppers in the oven for a light, smoky flavor that pairs well with the creaminess of an emulsified sauce. This relish can be made up to a day in advance, and would be lovely as a mezze with crostini, as an accompaniment to grilled fish, or alongside pork.

Preheat your oven to 400°F.

On a baking sheet, toss the bell peppers with 2 tablespoons olive oil until well coated. Roast in your oven, turning every 5 to 10 minutes, until each side has lightly blackened, about 30 minutes total.

Remove the peppers from your oven and set them aside in a large bowl covered with plastic wrap. Alternatively, you can wrap them in foil or seal them in a large covered container to trap the steam and cook the inside of the peppers. Let them sit in the sealed container until they've cooled to room temperature.

Once cool, tear off and discard the tops, seeds, and skin, reserving any roasting liquid that's left in the bowl. Tear the peppers into 1-inch-wide strips and place them in the bowl along with the roasting liquid. Set aside.

In a large pot on low heat, stir ¾ cup olive oil with the garlic and cook, stirring frequently, until the garlic just begins to brown, 5 to 7 minutes. Be careful to keep the heat low, stir often, and keep an eye on things—the high sugar content of garlic means it burns easily.

Once the garlic has lightly browned, remove the pot from the heat and stir in the red peppers, 1 tablespoon of the roasting liquid, and a pinch of salt. Return the pot to the stove on low heat. Cook, gently stirring often, until the oil turns the color of Dijon mustard and thickens to form a smooth, silky sauce, about 20 minutes. If after 20 minutes the oil shows no signs of thickening, try turning the heat up slightly and continue stirring until the oil emulsifies.

Stir in the vinegar, basil, and a healthy pinch of salt. Taste and add more salt if desired. Remove the pan from the heat and let the relish come to room temperature. Give everything a good stir before serving.

Serve immediately, or store the relish in an airtight container in your refrigerator for up to 2 days.

Pairs well with *"Let It Bleed" by The Rolling Stones*

Smoky Eggplant "Caviar"

Serves 4 to 6

1 large globe eggplant

1 small clove garlic, minced

½ cup plain Greek yogurt (whole milk strongly preferred)

¼ cup extra-virgin olive oil, plus more for drizzling

½ teaspoon garam masala (optional)

1 tablespoon freshly squeezed lemon juice, plus more to taste

Salt

2 tablespoons black or white sesame seeds, toasted (see page 80)

Think baba ghanoush, or, better yet, vegetable caviar. Eggplant can be intimidating, but this recipe asks you to burn it on purpose. This is my favorite method, where the nightshade is cooked naked over an open flame to impart a smoky flavor. Turn on your fan, open all the windows, and really burn it for longer than you think you should. A short amount of time yields an addictive spread that can be an elegant side or a quick snack. What's more—it gets better overnight.

With your gas stove (or even better—a hot charcoal fire!) on high, place the eggplant directly on the grate covering the burner. Use a pair of tongs to turn the eggplant until the entire surface is charred and completely black, 10 to 15 minutes total. It's okay for the eggplant to be firm and uncooked on the inside, just make sure the outer surface is charred on all sides.

Once fully charred and still hot, set the eggplant aside in a large bowl covered with plastic wrap. Alternatively, you can wrap it in foil or seal it in a large covered container to trap the steam and cook the eggplant's inside. Let sit in the sealed container until it's cooled to room temperature, at least 45 minutes. (Don't skimp on this step—if the eggplant is still warm it likely won't be cooked all the way through.)

Open the foil, discard any liquid that has formed, and remove the charred skin. The skin should peel off easily, but scrape off any lingering pieces with a knife. Cut off the top of the eggplant and slice the remaining flesh in half lengthwise. Spread it open on a cutting board and scoop out any seed pockets (don't worry about getting every seed).

Place the garlic on top of the eggplant and chop them together until a uniform paste forms with small pearls about the size of coarse sand. Transfer to a bowl and stir in the yogurt, olive oil, garam masala, and lemon juice. Season with salt to taste.

Pour the mixture into a serving bowl and drizzle olive oil on top. Finish with a sprinkling of sesame seeds.

It helps to know: This recipe requires a gas stove.

Serve immediately, or smooth out the top and cover it with olive oil. Store, covered in your refrigerator, for up to 4 days.

Pairs well with "Soul Kitchen" by Patti Smith

Baked Miso Eggplant

Serves 4 to 6

2 globe eggplants

White miso paste, at room temperature

I like to keep white miso paste stocked in my refrigerator because it's an easy trick: a store-bought seasoning packed with a ton of coveted umami flavor. I often add it to marinades or soup, but in this case, it's simply smeared onto a steamed eggplant and baked. The top transforms into a beautiful golden crust resembling a crème brûlée, and two simple ingredients yield an addicting snack or small plate to share.

Steam the eggplants. If you don't have a bamboo steaming basket or double boiler, there are a number of ways you can rig one—as long as you steam the eggplant without allowing it to touch the water. I don't have a steaming basket, so I put mine on top of a small upside-down heat-safe bowl sitting in a large pot of boiling water. Cover the pot with a tight-fitting lid and steam the eggplants until they're cooked through, about 30 minutes.

Set the eggplants aside to cool and firm, about 10 minutes.

Meanwhile, preheat your oven or toaster oven to 250°F. Line a baking sheet with aluminum foil.

Slice the eggplants in half lengthwise. Carefully spread a ¼- to ½-inch layer of miso paste on top of the cut side of the eggplant. Set the eggplants skin-side down on the foil-lined baking sheet and bake until the top has browned, about 30 minutes.

Remove the eggplants from your oven and let cool to room temperature. Using a sharp knife, trim off and discard the skin on both sides, and serve.

Pairs well with "Nothin' in the World Can Stop Me Worryin' 'Bout that Girl" by The Kinks

Savory Eggplant "Pâté"

Serves 6 to 8

2¼ pounds globe eggplants
(about 4), tops discarded

Extra-virgin olive oil

Salt and freshly ground black pepper

6 tablespoons crème fraîche

1 clove garlic, coarsely chopped

1 teaspoon cumin seeds

¼ teaspoon cayenne

7 eggs, at room temperature

1 loaf sourdough, cut into ½-inch
slices and toasted

**It helps to know: This recipe
requires a blender, a small
terrine or gratin dish, and
a second baking dish large
enough to hold the terrine.**

This vegetarian "pâté" is about as French as you can get: it's essentially an eggplant soufflé, complete with crème fraîche, and it's cooked in a bain-marie. It's classic but far from boring: the eggy, creamy eggplant spread puffs up like a loaf of bread, doing justice to one of my all-time favorite vegetables and all-time favorite cuisines. Though doubtful, if you do find yourself with leftovers, it keeps well covered in your refrigerator for up to 2 days.

Preheat your oven to 375°F.

Place the eggplants on individual sheets of aluminum foil, coat with olive oil, and sprinkle with a pinch each of salt and pepper. Wrap up the eggplants, set them on a baking sheet, and bake for 1 hour.

Remove the pan from your oven, leaving the oven on. Open the foil, slice the eggplants in half lengthwise, and let them cool to room temperature.

Once the eggplants are cool (don't skimp on this part or you'll cook the eggs!), discard any seed pockets (don't worry about getting every seed). Scoop the insides into a large bowl and discard the skin. Stir in the crème fraîche, garlic, cumin, cayenne, eggs, and a generous pinch each of salt and pepper. Pour the mixture into a food processor or blender, and blend on high speed until smooth.

Line the terrine with aluminum foil or parchment paper. Pour the eggplant mixture into the prepared dish. Set the terrine into the larger baking dish and fill the baking dish with water so it comes one-third of the way up the sides of the terrine. Bake the terrine sitting in water (called a bain-marie), for 1½ hours.

Remove the baking dish from your oven, remove the terrine from the baking dish, and let the pâté cool completely. Serve alongside the toasted sourdough.

Pairs well with "Ease Back" by The Meters

Potato Pancake with Horseradish Cream

Serves 4 to 6

POTATO PANCAKE

1 white onion, halved

1 clove garlic, finely chopped

1 tablespoon salt, plus more
for seasoning

Freshly ground black pepper

3 russet potatoes

¼ cup clarified butter (preferred),
olive oil, or sunflower oil

HORSERADISH CREAM

4 ounces cream cheese, at room
temperature

2 tablespoons freshly squeezed
lime juice

1 teaspoon rice vinegar

1 teaspoon jarred horseradish,
plus more to taste

Salt and freshly ground black pepper

½ cup heavy cream

I think I speak for most people when I say you really can't go wrong with a fried potato. This dish is essentially a gigantic potato latke, with a crispy and browned outside and a perfectly soft center (see photo, page 50). I would happily eat this on its own, but the horseradish cream is not to be missed: it gives just the right amount of kick to make this potato pancake difficult to forget.

Preheat your oven to 400°F.

To make the potato pancake, use the large side of a box grater to grate the cut side of the onion into a large bowl. Mix in the garlic, salt, and a generous pinch of pepper.

Peel the potatoes. Avoid the temptation to do this in advance—the onion's juices will soak into the potatoes and prevent them from oxidizing. (Don't cheat by soaking the potatoes in water; their starch is needed to thicken the pancake later.) Grate the peeled potatoes on the large side of a box grater. Use your hands to toss the onion mixture with the grated potatoes.

To remove their water, form a ball with the potato and onion mixture about the size of a tennis ball. Working in batches, squeeze out as much water as possible over the sink to discard. Transfer the potato and onion mixture to a new, dry bowl. Stir in a couple pinches of salt and pepper and use a fork to separate the pieces.

Heat the clarified butter in a large ovenproof pan on high heat until it's just starting to smoke. Add the potatoes and evenly spread them over the entire bottom of the pan to form a large pancake about ¾ inch thick. Use a spatula to scrape down and clean up the sides.

Let the pancake sit without moving until its edges start to brown. Once you see the bottom perimeter turn brown, put the pan in your oven for 20 minutes.

Remove the pan from your oven, and trace a spatula along the edges to loosen up the pancake. Set a plate on top of the pan, then turn the pan over so the pancake flips onto the plate with the bottom side facing up. Slide the pancake back into the pan with the bottom side still facing up. Top it with a healthy pinch of salt and return the pan to your oven. Bake for another 15 minutes. Remove the pan from your oven and transfer the pancake to a rack to cool to room temperature (don't let it cool in the pan or it will get soggy).

Meanwhile, to make the horseradish cream, stir together the cream cheese, lime juice, vinegar, horseradish, and a pinch each of salt and pepper in a large bowl. Use a wooden spoon or spatula to stir vigorously until the ingredients are combined and the cream cheese is light and fluffy. Add the heavy cream and use a whisk to whip until the cream thickens and develops soft peaks. In other words, when you lift the whisk out of the bowl, the mixture holds its shape for a second or two before melting back into itself.

When the potato pancake has cooled to room temperature, slice it like a pizza. Add a dollop of the horseradish cream to each slice and serve.

Pairs well with "E.S.P." by Buzzcocks

⟩ Clockwise from top: Mushrooms al Horno with Crusty Bread (page 54); Raw Fava, Chickpea & Tahini Hummus (page 35); Guacamole with Pomegranate (page 53); Salmon Rillettes (page 52); and Potato Pancake with Horseradish Cream (page 48)

Salmon Rillettes

Serves 4 to 6

5 ounces sushi-grade salmon

¼ cup butter, softened

¼ cup Mother-Sauce Mayo (page 17)
    or store-bought mayonnaise

1 (5-ounce) piece cold-smoked
    salmon, skin removed and
    finely diced

Zest and juice of ½ lemon

5 tablespoons finely chopped chives

1 teaspoon salt

1 teaspoon freshly ground
    black pepper

1 baguette, cut into ½-inch slices
    and toasted

I learned this recipe many years ago and I revisit it often because I still adore it. The combination of smoked salmon and crudo makes it sing. It's also incredibly easy to prepare ahead of time and store in your refrigerator, making it a perfect low-stress small plate for your table. (See photo, previous page.)

To prepare the raw salmon, slice it into thin strips and place it in your freezer for 10 minutes. Remove and finely dice the strips.

Meanwhile, whisk the butter in a large bowl until it's fluffy. Whisk in the mayonnaise until combined. Stir in the smoked salmon, raw salmon, lemon zest and juice, the chives, salt, and pepper.

Scoop the rillettes into a serving dish and serve immediately with the sliced baguette. Alternatively, store it in a covered container in your refrigerator for up to 1 day. Let it come to room temperature before serving.

Pairs well with "Three Cigarettes in an Ashtray" by Patsy Cline

Guacamole with Pomegranate

Serves 4 to 6

3 ripe avocados

Juice of 3 or 4 limes

1 small red onion, quartered and
    thinly sliced

½ clove garlic, finely chopped

2 serrano chiles, seeded and
    finely minced

1 jalapeño, seeded and finely minced

½ teaspoon smoked pimento powder
    or other smoked chile powder

1 cup loosely packed cilantro leaves,
    finely chopped

Salt and freshly ground black pepper

1 tablespoon pomegranate syrup

1 teaspoon black sesame seeds,
    toasted (page 80)

Seeds of 1 small pomegranate

Everyone has a guacamole recipe, especially in California. This is mine. (See photo, page 51.)

Halve the avocados, remove their pits (save one for storage!), and scoop the flesh into a large bowl. Add the juice from 3 limes along with the onion, garlic, serrano chiles, jalapeño, pimento powder, cilantro, and a generous pinch each of salt and pepper.

Mash with a fork until the ingredients form a rough paste but still retain some texture. Guacamole with chunks and different textures is much more interesting, so make sure not to over-mash the avocados. Taste and adjust the salt and lime levels, if necessary. Place in your refrigerator for 30 minutes to allow the onion to soften.

Scoop the guacamole into your serving bowl. Drizzle with the pomegranate syrup, and sprinkle with the sesame and pomegranate seeds to finish.

Serve immediately, or store covered for up to 1 day in your refrigerator with the avocado pit half submerged in the dip to prevent it from oxidizing.

Pairs well with "*Alegria*" *by Elia y Elizabeth*

Mushrooms al Horno with Crusty Bread

Serves 4

2 pounds mushrooms (a mixed variety of your choice)

2 cloves garlic, finely chopped

¼ cup tightly packed fresh flat-leaf parsley leaves, finely chopped

2 tablespoons dry white wine

¼ cup extra-virgin olive oil

Salt

1 teaspoon sherry vinegar

2 (½-inch-thick) slices sourdough bread, halved and toasted

These baked ("al horno") mushrooms are inspired by a Basque dish. The mushrooms kick out their water, which combines with the wine, garlic, vinegar, and herbs to make a very flavorful sauce. This dish is super straightforward (just mix some things together and throw them in your oven); my only advice: don't soak the mushrooms in water to clean them or they'll soak up too much liquid and ruin the rich, mushroomy sauce.

Preheat your oven to 400°F.

Clean the mushrooms with a damp towel and cut them into bite-size pieces.

Put the mushrooms in a large bowl and stir in the garlic, parsley, white wine, olive oil, and two healthy pinches of salt until combined. Pour the mixture into a baking dish large enough to hold the mushrooms in a single layer and bake for 30 minutes.

Remove the dish from your oven and stir in the sherry vinegar.

Divide the toasted bread among serving plates. Spoon the mushrooms and their juices over the bread and serve.

Pairs well with "Stolen Moments" by Oliver Nelson

Farinata

Serves 4

120 grams chickpea flour

3 grams salt

360 grams tepid water

45 grams extra-virgin olive oil, plus more for coating the pan

Freshly ground black pepper

Flaky sea salt

Finely grated Parmigiano-Reggiano, Pecorino Romano, or soft Gorgonzola dolce (optional)

It helps to know: This recipe requires a scale and a shallow pan 10 to 12 inches wide. A paella pan, cast-iron skillet, or crêpe pan works well.

This is one of the few recipes for which I ask you to buy a $10 scale because the measurements need to be accurate, but it's worth it. Farinata (essentially a chickpea pancake) is a more recent obsession of mine. As such, I've spent the better part of the past year perfecting my recipe at home. The edges are crispy with a soft, almost custard-like, center, which leaves you with a difficult choice between which texture you like best. This is clearly not a dairy- or gluten-free cookbook, but this recipe (excluding the optional cheese addition) happens to be both.

Sift the chickpea flour into a large bowl, then sift into another large bowl once more (it's very important to remove any lumps and sifting twice usually does the trick). Sift in the salt and stir to combine.

Add 180 grams of the tepid water and whisk until smooth. Add the remaining 180 grams tepid water and whisk until a very thin batter forms that is smooth and free of any lumps. Set the bowl aside, uncovered, at room temperature for 1½ hours to let the batter hydrate.

Preheat your oven to 450°F.

A layer of foam will have risen to the surface of the dough. Skim off and discard the foam, then whisk in the olive oil and pepper to taste (I like a lot).

Add enough olive oil to the pan to fully coat the bottom. Carefully slide the middle rack partly out of your oven and place the pan on the rack. Pour the batter into the pan without removing the pan from the rack—you want to move the batter as little as possible once it's poured. Sprinkle a generous amount of flaky sea salt across the top, then slide the rack back into your oven, being careful to disturb the pan as little as possible.

Bake until the top is nicely browned, 14 to 16 minutes. Remove the pan from your oven and let the farinata cool for 3 minutes.

Top with Parmigiano-Reggiano or Pecorino Romano to taste. Or, if you're feeling decadent, spread some soft Gorgonzola dolce on top. Carefully slice the farinata into 4 pieces in the pan like a pizza and treat it as a thick crêpe, eating it with your hands (like me) or with a fork and knife.

Pairs well with "Shake Your Hips" by Slim Harpo

Savory Strawberry Biscuits

Makes 9 to 12 sandwiches

BISCUITS

1½ cups all-purpose flour,
    plus more for dusting

1 teaspoon baking powder

¼ teaspoon baking soda

1 teaspoon sugar

½ teaspoon salt

½ cup butter, frozen

Zest of 1 lemon

¾ cup crème fraîche

¾ cup strawberries, washed, hulled
    (see page 71), and thinly sliced

1 tablespoon butter, melted

FILLINGS

Jam of your choice (I like rhubarb,
    strawberry, or apricot)

Manchego cheese with prosciutto,
    Gouda with Serrano ham, or Brie
    with boiled ham

I'm not sure whether these biscuits should be considered breakfast, lunch, or a snack, but they're delicious at any time of day. My advice is to work quickly with the dough: it will get more difficult to handle as it warms up.

I like a few different combinations for the inside of the biscuit sandwich, but feel free to get creative. Just look for something fatty, something salty, and something sweet—a meat, a cheese, and a jam.

Preheat your oven to 450°F. Line a baking sheet with parchment paper and put it in your freezer to chill.

Sift the flour into a large bowl to remove any clumps. Sift in the baking powder, baking soda, sugar, and salt and stir to combine. Using the large side of a box grater, grate the frozen butter into the flour mixture. Stir in the lemon zest, then the crème fraîche. Don't worry—the mixture will be chunky and not dough-like at this point.

Stir in the strawberries and begin working the mixture with your hands, pinching and turning as the butter melts and the strawberries burst, until everything eventually comes together to form a dough. Be patient; it will take some time for the butter to melt and may feel for a few minutes like it's not working.

Form the dough into a ball and dust a large work surface and rolling pin with flour. Set the dough on your work surface and use your palm to flatten its top. Dust the dough with more flour, then roll it into a rough square about 1½ inches thick. Cut the dough into 2-inch squares, and space the squares evenly on the prepared baking sheet.

Brush the tops of the squares with the melted butter and bake until they're nicely browned and cooked through, about 22 minutes. Remove the pan from your oven and transfer the biscuits to a wire rack to cool to room temperature.

Slice the biscuits in half. Spread the jam on one side and put the cheese on the other. Push a couple of slices of ham into the jam and push the two halves together to make a sandwich. Serve.

Pairs well with "I Love What You Do to Me" by Ike & Tina Turner

Corn Cakes with Smoked Salmon

¾ cup crème fraîche

1 tablespoon Dijon mustard

2 eggs

1 scant cup all-purpose flour, sifted

2 cups heavy whipping cream

2 teaspoons Tabasco sauce

Kernels from 4 ears of corn
(see page 72)

Salt

About ½ cup butter

8 ounces cold-smoked salmon

1 red onion, thinly sliced

1 bunch green onions, trimmed,
white and tender green parts
thinly sliced

**It helps to know: This recipe
requires a 4- to 5-inch pan
(ideally, a crêpe pan) and
a blender.**

These corn crêpes are savory meets sweet meets breakfast meets good-all-day-long—you really can't go wrong with smoked fish on a pancake.

Preheat your oven to 375°F.

In a small bowl, whisk together the crème fraîche and Dijon mustard. Set aside.

In a large bowl, whisk the eggs into the flour. Whisk in the cream and Tabasco until combined. Stir in the corn and a couple pinches of salt. Add the mixture to a blender and blend minimally on low speed, ensuring some whole kernels remain.

In a small ovenproof pan on medium heat, warm about 1 tablespoon of the butter, tilting to coat the pan as it melts. Pour enough batter into the pan so it reaches the edges and makes a ¾-inch-thick pancake. Let it sit until the batter starts to bubble around the edges. Once bubbling, put the pan in your oven and bake until the pancake is cooked through, about 4 minutes.

Trace a spatula along the edges of the pan to loosen up the pancake's perimeter. Set a plate on top of the pan, then turn the pan over so the pancake flips onto the plate with the bottom side facing up. Slide the pancake back into the pan, with the bottom side still facing up, and return the pan to the stove on medium heat.

Continue cooking until both sides are golden brown, about 4 minutes more. Remove from the pan and set aside to cool to room temperature. Repeat with the remaining batter, replenishing the butter as necessary.

Top the corn cakes with a dollop of the crème fraîche and Dijon mixture, and some salmon, red onion, and green onions. Serve immediately.

Pairs well with "Mojo Hand" by Lightnin' Hopkins

SALADS, FRUITS + SOUPS, TO START

At my restaurant Manresa, we don't turn tables, which means that if you're seated at table twenty-five, you're the only person who will sit at that table for the entire evening. You've reserved it: it's your table. We don't get many walk-ins (people usually plan ahead for these kinds of dinners), so we know exactly how many guests will pass through the doors on any given night—give or take a couple—before service begins.

We keep a pretty quiet kitchen so the chefs and cooks can hear what they're supposed to be making, and the front-of-house can hear where they're supposed to be going. It's a delicate system. Stepping into the kitchen at any given moment, you should only hear the voice of the expediter, the person who stands at the pass directing service, and the call back. The call back is the crucial repetition of what the expediter has just said by the person with whom they're speaking. It means "heard, understood, on it." This can be as simple as, "Birthday cake to table 31," or as important as, "P-two on table 36 has a shellfish allergy." The expediter hears the call back, sees the modified dish carefully picked up with the food runner's left hand, and watches them walk through the swinging doors. The rest is left to a highly capable staff and their shared trust.

Aside from the voice of the expediter, the call back, and the food being prepared, there's one sound that I will probably hear long after I've retired somewhere far away from any restaurant kitchen: tickets being printed. All night, as guests are seated, the ticket machine is running, making its distinctive, high-pitched, back-and-forth whine of ink hitting moving paper. Come 9:30 p.m., the expediter has made it through the bulk of the tickets and is anxiously awaiting the soothing sound of the last ticket coming through the printer. He or she tears it out of the machine and, with enthusiasm, projects, "ALL IN!" The chefs, the polisher, the captains, the runners, the porters, and anyone else who happens to be in the kitchen during that magical moment calls back, "ALL IN!" For that last table, the night is just beginning, but for the rest of us, it's a signal of the end. The bulk of the night's work is behind us; we take a breath and relax into doing what we love: feeding our remaining guests a phenomenal meal. And so it goes, night after night: the chaotic repetition of a fine-dining restaurant.

The dishes in this chapter represent the part of the night when your guests move from drinking and snacking on their feet to being

seated at the table—such as it may be. That transition brings a certain energy: the exuberant feeling of your prep work being finished, your friends being seated, and the anticipation of a very good meal to come.

These recipes capture that all-in feeling, the excitement of being able to enjoy the fruits of your labor. The salads are interactive: ingredients are torn and dipped, and pits are spit out, as with my Petit Aioli with Canned Tuna (page 67). Or the lettuce is cooked and savory, as in my Braised Lettuce & Smoky Bacon (page 83) or blanched and blended, like my Lettuce Vichyssoise (page 99). Most of the dishes are highly seasonal, be it Creamed Corn & Garden Tomatoes (page 72) in the summer or Persimmon, Pomegranate & Roquefort Salad (page 75) in the winter. All are relatively low maintenance: it's the beginning of the end, and your time to sit down, too.

My hope is that, with the help of these dishes, you'll give the signal that the meal is about to start, the last guest will sit down at your table, and you'll think to yourself, "ALL IN!" Like me, you'll take a breath and relax, ready to share a meal together. This is cooking for fun.

A Riviera Salad

Serves 8

1 pound small tomatoes (Early Girl or Roma preferred), quartered

Salt

12 ounces fingerling potatoes

1 pound raw fava beans

3 heads Little Gem lettuce

14 basil leaves

1 clove garlic, halved

2 green bell peppers, stemmed, seeded, and thinly sliced

1 small red onion, thinly sliced

2 small cucumbers, peeled and cut into ¼-inch slices

½ cup pitted Niçoise olives

8 ounces canned solid tuna packed in oil, drained

3 eggs, hard-boiled (see page 113), peeled, and halved lengthwise

Freshly ground black pepper

⅓ cup extra-virgin olive oil

The Niçoise salad comes with its own baggage: people have a lot of opinions about what should (and shouldn't) be included. This is my take, which veers from tradition but keeps the summer flavors of the Riviera that have made the Niçoise such a classic.

Spread the tomatoes on a plate in a single layer. Sprinkle with a generous pinch of salt and set aside for at least 30 minutes as you prepare the rest of the ingredients.

Cover the potatoes with cold water in a large pot. Add 1 tablespoon salt and turn the heat to medium. Simmer, uncovered, until the potatoes are soft, about 20 minutes. Drain and set aside to cool. Once cool, cut them in half lengthwise.

Blanch the fava beans by dunking them in boiling water for 30 seconds. Drain and run cold water over them to stop the cooking process. Pop the beans out of their pod and use a knife to peel and discard the outer skin.

Remove the outer leaves from the lettuce and trim the very bottom stem, being careful not to trim off too much or they'll break apart. Cut each head in half lengthwise, then in half lengthwise once more to make wedges.

Tear half of the basil leaves into bite-size pieces.

To assemble the salad, rub the cut side of the garlic clove over your serving platter's surface. Scatter the Little Gems, fingerlings, fava beans, bell peppers, onion, cucumbers, and olives over the platter, finding space in all the gaps. Add the tuna, breaking it into bite-size pieces. Top with the eggs, torn basil, the tomatoes, and a healthy pinch of black pepper. Cover the platter with plastic wrap and chill in your refrigerator for at least 30 minutes, or up to 2 hours.

Finely chop the remaining basil leaves. In a small bowl, whisk the basil into the olive oil, cover, and chill in your refrigerator along with the salad.

Just before serving, drizzle with the dressing and a pinch of salt.

Pairs well with "Time" by Shirley Ann Lee

Petit Aioli with Canned Tuna

Serves 6

1 pound fingerling potatoes

1 tablespoon salt, plus more for seasoning

2 bunches baby carrots (ideally rainbow), tops removed and peeled

2 fennel bulbs, bottoms trimmed

2 cloves garlic

3 small tomatoes (Early Girl or Roma preferred)

1 large red bell pepper, stemmed and seeded

1 zucchini

1 egg yolk, at room temperature

½ cup extra-virgin olive oil

Juice from ½ lemon

4 eggs, hard-boiled (see page 113), peeled, and halved lengthwise

1 cup green olives

7 ounces canned solid tuna packed in oil, drained

Freshly ground black pepper

I love this dish because it's a fresh, light way to start a meal, but also because it's pretty: the olives, rainbow carrots, and varying vegetables arrange themselves into interesting shapes and pockets to show off their natural vibrancy. It's also an easy way to serve a lot of people, and it can be made in advance. Serve this on a big platter family style, ideally outdoors, with a bottle or two of rosé.

Cover the potatoes in cold water in a large pot. Add the salt and turn the heat to medium. Simmer, uncovered, until the potatoes are soft, about 30 minutes. Drain and let the potatoes cool, setting one aside for the aioli. Once cooled to room temperature, cut them in half lengthwise.

Meanwhile, blanch the carrots and fennel. Bring a large pot of water to a boil on high heat and set a large bowl of cold water next to your stove. Once boiling, add a pinch of salt. Dunk the carrots and fennel in the boiling water for 30 seconds, then use a large slotted spoon to immediately plunge them into the cold water. The cold water stops the vegetables from cooking and keeps their bright, raw color. Leave the carrots whole and quarter the fennel. Set aside.

Cook the garlic in the boiling water for 2 minutes. Drain and run cold water over the garlic to halt the cooking process. Set aside to cool to room temperature.

Cut the tomatoes in half lengthwise, then in half lengthwise again to make wedges. Cut the bell pepper into quarters. Discard the zucchini's end, cut it into 2-inch lengths, then cut the pieces into quarters. Set aside.

Peel the skin from the reserved fingerling potato (don't use a warm potato or it will cook the egg).

Using a mortar and pestle, smash the softened garlic to form a paste. (If you don't have a mortar and pestle, use a hand whisk, but finely chop the softened garlic and smash the cooked potato with a fork before you begin.) Add the potato and continue to smash until combined. Add the egg yolk and continue to smash and stir. Slowly drizzle in the olive oil, continuing to stir aggressively. Add a few drops at a time at first, being careful not to add too much oil at once or the sauce will break. When the sauce becomes too thick to stir, add a few drops of cold water. Continue with this process, adding cold water as necessary to thin, until all of the oil has been incorporated. Season with salt to taste, and then stir in the lemon juice.

continued

To serve, arrange the tomatoes, vegetables, eggs, and olives attractively in a large bowl or serving dish. Sometimes I layer the vegetables randomly, sometimes I group like things together. Get creative and have fun. Use your hands to break up the tuna into large pieces and evenly spread it on top of the vegetables. Very lightly salt and pepper the entire dish. Serve alongside small bowls of the aioli and your best olive oil.

Pairs well with "Like a Ship" by Pastor T. L. Barrett and the Youth for Christ Choir

Roast Fig & Pancetta Salad with Goat Cheese

Serves 4 to 6

1 small head radicchio

2 tablespoons extra-virgin olive oil

1 tablespoon balsamic vinegar

Salt and freshly ground black pepper

6 fresh figs, halved

6 ounces pancetta, thinly sliced

1 (8- to 10-ounce) goat cheese log, cut into 6 (¼-inch) slices

This cooked fruit and lettuce salad is sweet and salty and creamy and delicious. It goes well with roast or grilled meat in the summertime, or, since it's fairly filling by itself, alongside a simple arugula salad with a classic dressing (see page 24) for a double-salad kind of night.

Preheat your oven to 375°F.

Slice the radicchio in half and remove and discard its core. Vertically slice each half into ½-inch slices. Place the radicchio in a bowl and toss with the olive oil, vinegar, and a pinch each of salt and pepper until combined.

Spread the radicchio evenly on the bottom of an ovenproof casserole dish large enough to hold all of the figs in a single layer. Set aside.

Wrap the figs in the pancetta slices, then set them on top of the radicchio. Bake until the pancetta begins to crisp, 9 to 11 minutes.

Remove the dish from your oven and set the goat cheese slices on top of each fig. Return the dish to your oven and bake until the cheese has softened and warmed through, 1 to 2 minutes. Serve immediately.

Pairs well with "She Lied" by Rockin' Ramrods

Tomato Salad with Anchovy & Basil

Serves 4 to 6

8 heirloom tomatoes,
　cut into ¾-inch slices

12 ounces water-packed burrata

Leaves from 1 bunch basil

¼ cup extra-virgin olive oil

1 tablespoon flaky sea salt

12 anchovy fillets (oil-packed),
　rinsed and drained

1 tablespoon red wine vinegar

Freshly ground black pepper
　(optional)

This dish is best served during the height of summer, when tomatoes speak for themselves with very little embellishment. Salt draws out the tomato's juices, combining with the burrata's cream and the olive oil to make its own dressing. All this salad needs is the smallest touch of vinegar. You could leave it at that, sure, but in my opinion, this is infinitely better when garnished with basil and—best of all—little fish.

Spread the tomato slices across your serving platter. Use a tablespoon to scoop the burrata and spread it attractively on top of and in between the tomato slices.

Stack the basil leaves. Use kitchen scissors to cut bite-size pieces of basil over the top of the dish, scattering the pieces across the tomatoes and burrata. Drizzle everything with the olive oil, then sprinkle with the salt. Cover the platter loosely with plastic wrap and set it aside to marinate at room temperature for at least 30 minutes or up to 1 hour.

Lay the anchovies on top of the tomatoes. Use a spoon to very lightly drizzle the vinegar on top: about 1 drop per tomato slice. Season with pepper to taste and serve, scooping up the juices that pool at the bottom of the serving dish.

Pairs well with *"Pour Faire le Portrait d'un Oiseau" by Yves Montand*

Tomato & Strawberry Salad with Feta & Olives

Serves 4 to 6

1 pound fully ripe small tomatoes
(such as Early Girl, heirloom,
or cherry)

8 ounces strawberries, washed, hulled
(see below), and halved lengthwise

2 tablespoons red wine vinegar

4 tablespoons extra-virgin olive oil

8 ounces feta cheese packed in brine,
torn into large pieces

½ cup pitted or unpitted Taggiasca
or Niçoise olives

Flaky sea salt and freshly ground
black pepper

As with my Strawberry Gazpacho "Smoothie" (page 91), this dish highlights my attraction to the affinity a tomato shares with a strawberry, and how they can be used interchangeably. Here, I mix them together for a simple summer tomato salad with a small surprise. I like spitting out the pits when I eat olives (I make sure to warn my guests), but you can also buy them pitted—it's just not as much fun in my opinion.

Cut the tomatoes to be roughly the same size as the halved strawberries. If you're using cherry tomatoes, cut them in half. If you're using another small tomato variety, quarter them.

In a small bowl, whisk the red wine vinegar and olive oil with 1 tablespoon of the brine from the feta.

Spread the tomatoes on a serving plate. Top with the strawberries, olives, and feta. Drizzle the dressing over the top and finish with salt and pepper to taste. Serve immediately.

Pairs well with "Circles" by Les Fleur de Lys

HOW TO WASH & HULL STRAWBERRIES

Because strawberry seeds are on the outside of the fruit, they tend to be excellent collectors of dirt. To clean them, fill a large bowl with cold water. Dump the berries in and let them sit in the water while you remove and discard their tops. Set the hulled strawberries aside on a paper towel to drain, then pat them dry before using.

Creamed Corn & Garden Tomatoes

Serves 6 to 8

2 pounds heirloom tomatoes
   of assorted shapes, sizes,
   and colors

½ pint cherry tomatoes,
   halved lengthwise

Flaky sea salt

Extra-virgin olive oil

2 tablespoons sherry vinegar

Freshly ground black pepper

6 large basil leaves (opal basil,
   Thai basil, or as many varieties
   as you can find), plus more
   for garnish

2 cups heavy whipping cream

Kernels from 3 large ears corn
   (see below)

HOW TO KERNEL CORN

Fold a paper towel into quarters and set it at the bottom of a large bowl. This prevents the cob from slipping while you cut off the kernels.

Place the flat side of the stem on the paper towel and hold the ear upright with your nondominant hand. Cut off the kernels using a sharp knife. Once you've removed the kernels on all sides, remove the paper towel, flip the knife over and press the dull side along the empty cob to force out the corn's juices.

This "salad" uses simple summer ingredients in an interesting way: the cool, raw tomatoes and warm creamy corn give a nice contrast, and, best of all, it celebrates the diversity of produce available in what I wish were the only season. Use as many different varieties of basil and tomatoes as you can find.

Cut the heirloom tomatoes into bite-size portions of all different shapes. Get creative!

Spread the cherry and heirloom tomatoes evenly onto your serving dish. Sprinkle with salt, a drizzle of olive oil, the sherry vinegar, and a couple pinches of pepper.

Cut the basil into a chiffonade, which is a fancy-sounding name for a very simple cut. Stack the basil leaves on top of each other and roll them together lengthwise like a cigar. Slice thinly to make matchstick-size strips.

Top the tomatoes with the basil, cover the entire dish in plastic wrap, and set aside to marinate at room temperature for 30 minutes.

Meanwhile, reduce the cream in a large, uncovered pot on medium heat, stirring frequently to prevent burning. After about 10 minutes, the cream should have reduced by half and thickened to a frosting-like consistency. Turn the heat to low to maintain a gentle simmer and add the corn and a healthy pinch each of salt and pepper. Simmer, uncovered, for 5 minutes. The corn will eventually release its water and thin out the cream.

Before serving, taste a tomato piece to check its salt level. Top with another pinch of flaky sea salt, if necessary. Scoop the hot corn over the tomatoes and garnish with a variety of basil leaves. Divide into bowls, scooping up the juices from the bottom of the dish and drizzling them over the top, and serve.

Pairs well with "These Foolish Things (Remind Me of You)" by Stan Getz

Persimmon, Pomegranate & Roquefort Salad

Serves 4

4 Belgian endives

Seeds of 1 large pomegranate

⅓ cup extra-virgin olive oil

1 tablespoon freshly squeezed lime juice

4 crisp Fuyu persimmons, thinly sliced

6 ounces Roquefort (or other blue cheese), crumbled

There's a lot to praise in this vibrant winter salad. The bright orange persimmons and sharp blue cheese combined with crisp green endives make a beautifully colorful, flavorful, and texture-rich dish. What's more, it's always such a welcome pleasure to have a ripe fruit in the colder months. Be sure to use Fuyu persimmons (the shorter, rounder variety), as they don't have the tannic quality of their cousins.

Remove the outer brown leaves from the endives. Slice off the tops and stems and break the spears apart into cups.

Using a mortar and pestle, the bottom of a wine bottle, end of a rolling pin, or anything you have on hand that's sturdy and has a flat bottom, crush about half of the pomegranate seeds in a large bowl, mashing them enough to release their juices but keeping about half of the seeds intact. Add the olive oil and lime juice and whisk to combine.

Arrange the endives and persimmon slices on your serving dish. Top with the pomegranate seed and olive oil mixture, then the cheese. Serve.

Pairs well with *"Out of Time" by Chris Farlowe*

Citrus & Almond Salad

Serves 4

1 blood orange

2 oranges (I like Cara Cara)

1 grapefruit (I like Oro Blanco)

1 head frisée

1 jalapeño, halved

¼ cup extra-virgin olive oil

Freshly squeezed juice from ½ lemon

Freshly squeezed juice from ½ lime

2 tablespoons whole blanched
   almonds, lightly toasted
   (see page 83)

1 tablespoon fresh flat-leaf parsley
   leaves for garnish

Finely grated Parmigiano-Reggiano
   or Pecorino Romano

This winter salad is not only good-looking and easy to make, but it also showcases one of my biggest food obsessions: citrus. You can use almost any citrus (even limes and lemons in small quantities), as long as they're ripe and juicy. If you can't find frisée, thinly slice a fennel bulb as a substitute.

Peel the oranges and grapefruit using a sharp knife, then thinly slice each horizontally, discarding any large seeds.

Discard the tough outer leaves of the frisée until you're left with the delicate white heart. Tear the heart into bite-size pieces, rinse with cold water, and pat dry.

Rub your serving dish with the jalapeño. Arrange the citrus across the platter, alternating between the oranges and the grapefruit, then top with the frisée. Drizzle with the olive oil, lemon juice, and lime juice, then cover the platter with plastic wrap and set in your refrigerator to marinate in its own juices for at least 30 minutes, or up to 2 hours.

Once the citrus has marinated, top it with the almonds, parsley, and Parmigiano-Reggiano to taste. Serve, scooping up the juices and oil that have gathered at the bottom of the platter.

Pairs well with "Pepper Pot" by Art Pepper

Brussels Sprouts with Cider & Goat Cheese

Serves 6 to 8

2½ cups apple cider

1¼ cups turbinado or raw light
  brown sugar

1 pound brussels sprouts

Extra-virgin olive oil

2 ounces pancetta, cut into
  ¼-inch slices

2 shallots, thinly sliced lengthwise

Salt

1 tablespoon apple cider vinegar

1 tablespoon freshly squeezed
  lime juice

8 ounces fresh goat cheese, broken
  into bite-size pieces

1 crisp, acidic apple (such as Granny
  Smith or Honeycrisp), thinly sliced

Freshly ground black pepper

I serve these brussels sprouts every year at Thanksgiving, but they would also make a delicious side dish for any fall or winter dinner. The sweetness of an apple cider glaze balances the acidity of the vinegar, and the creamy cheese and salty bacon bring everything together nicely. Feel free to leave off the pancetta to appease your vegetarian friends.

First, make a glaze. In a small pot on high heat, combine the cider and turbinado sugar and bring to a boil, stirring often, until the sugar dissolves, about 5 minutes. Turn down the heat and simmer, uncovered, until the mixture reduces to a syrupy consistency, about 30 minutes. Remove the pan from the heat and let the glaze cool completely.

Meanwhile, trim off the end of each brussels sprout, letting the outer leaves fall off. Peel off and discard any dark leaves that are attached to the main bulb. Cut each sprout in half, place each half flat-side down, and thinly slice lengthwise.

In a large pan on medium heat, warm 1 teaspoon olive oil. Add the pancetta, turn the heat to low, and cook until the pancetta is crispy and golden, about 4 minutes. Strain the pancetta over a bowl to reserve its fat, then lay it on a paper towel to drain.

Pour the reserved fat back into the pan and turn the heat to medium. Add 1 tablespoon olive oil, the shallots, brussels sprouts, and a pinch of salt. Cook, stirring often, until the shallots soften and the brussels sprouts start to caramelize, about 7 minutes.

Add the apple cider vinegar and lime juice and stir until dissolved. Stir in the pancetta and cook for 1 minute more to warm everything through.

Remove the pan from the heat and pour everything into a large bowl to cool to room temperature.

Once cooled, add ¼ cup of the glaze and stir to combine. Taste and add more glaze, if desired. (Store any leftover glaze, covered, in your refrigerator for up to 1 week. It's great drizzled on vanilla ice cream.) Top with the goat cheese and sliced apple, and season with salt and pepper to taste. Serve.

Pairs well with "So You Want to Be a Rock 'n' Roll Star" by Sun Dragon

Spicy Sesame Cucumber with Avocado

Serves 4 to 6

2 small English cucumbers

Salt

1 small red onion

1 large avocado, peeled, seeded, and coarsely chopped

2 small jalapeños, seeded and finely minced

2 tablespoons black or white sesame seeds, toasted (see below)

¼ cup toasted sesame oil (cold-pressed preferred)

¼ cup rice vinegar

HOW TO TOAST SESAME SEEDS

Spread the seeds evenly in a cold dry pan. Set the pan on the stove and turn the heat to medium-low. Swirl the pan to prevent the seeds from burning.

Toast, swirling frequently, until they are fragrant and take on some color. The seeds will continue to brown, so be sure to remove them from the pan just before they're done.

White sesame seeds are easy—you'll see them start to change color. If you're using black sesame seeds, you have to rely on your nose. When they start to become aromatic, they're finished. Set aside on a plate to cool.

I love, love, love this fragrant salad. I've done different takes on it throughout the years, but it dates back to being a young line cook in New York City. A whimsical take on guacamole, which itself makes it worth a try, it's fantastic alone or with chips, and even better when topped with sliced, marinated fish, ceviche-style.

Trim off the ends of the cucumbers and halve them lengthwise, then cut the halves in half lengthwise once more. Scrape out the exposed seeds. Cut each quarter into ¼-inch slices. In a colander, toss the cucumbers with a pinch of salt. Set the colander in your sink for 30 minutes. The salt will force the cucumbers to expel their excess water. Transfer the cucumbers to a paper towel to dry.

Meanwhile, halve the onion lengthwise, then slice each half into thin half-moons. Soak the slices in a bowl of ice water for 10 minutes to crisp and tone down their raw flavor. Transfer to a paper towel to dry.

In a medium bowl, stir together the avocado and cucumber. Add half of the red onion slices, the jalapeños, 1 tablespoon of the sesame seeds, and the sesame oil. Mash the ingredients with a fork, gently breaking up the avocado into a chunky paste. Be careful to not overdo it—some texture is essential to a pleasant guacamole.

Stir in the rice vinegar and season with salt to taste. Top with the remaining red onion and 1 tablespoon sesame seeds. Serve immediately.

Pairs well with "La Llorona" by Chavela Vargas

Braised Lettuce & Smoky Bacon

Serves 6 to 8

3 heads romaine lettuce

4 ounces skin-on smoked slab bacon or bacon slices

Salt

3 tablespoons extra-virgin olive oil

¼ cup dry white wine

1 clove garlic, smashed

Freshly ground black pepper

½ cup toasted walnuts (see below), coarsely chopped

HOW TO TOAST NUTS

I don't like to toast nuts in a pan on the stove because the heat comes only from the bottom. If you're not continuously shaking the pan, they burn. Plus, toasting nuts in the oven is incredibly easy.

Preheat your oven to 350°F and spread the nuts on a baking sheet in a single layer. Bake, shaking the pan occasionally, until they're toasted. The time this takes will depend on the size of the nut. Pine nuts are easy; you can see them turn golden when they're done. For others, you have to trust your nose. When the oils contained in the nuts become fragrant, and you can smell them toasting, they're finished.

I feel strongly that lettuce should be used for more than just salad: don't be afraid to cook it. Smoky bacon is obviously delicious, but the cooked, wilted lettuce is what shines in this dish. I much prefer skin-on slab bacon, but I know it can be hard to find. Ideally you can get your hands on a whole piece of pork belly so you can cut large pieces, but sliced bacon will work in a pinch (in which case, there's no need to boil it, just cook it with the olive oil until crispy).

Preheat your oven to 375°F.

Discard the outer leaves of the romaine bunches and slice off the tops.

If using slab bacon, cover it with cold water in a small pot and turn the heat to high. Bring to a simmer, skimming off the scum that forms at the surface. Turn down the heat to maintain a gentle simmer and cook, uncovered, for 30 minutes. Drain over a bowl to reserve the broth and set the bacon aside on a paper towel to cool to room temperature. Once cooled, discard its skin, then cut the flesh into pieces about 1 inch long by ½ inch wide.

Bring a large pot of water to a boil on high heat. Once boiling, add a small pinch of salt. Dunk the lettuce in the boiling water until it wilts, about 15 seconds. Remove and halve lengthwise. (I don't dunk the lettuce in cold water as it will turn brown.)

In a medium pan on low heat, stir together the olive oil and bacon. Continue stirring until the bacon starts to crisp, about 10 minutes. Push the bacon to the edges of the pan and lay the blanched lettuce, cut-side down, in the center. Sprinkle with a small pinch of salt and cook until the cut side of the lettuce has nicely browned, 5 to 7 minutes.

Add the white wine, garlic, ¾ cup of the reserved bacon broth or water, and a pinch of pepper. Cover and cook for 5 minutes, shaking the pan every so often to prevent sticking.

Use tongs to flip the lettuce onto its other side. Replace the cover and cook for another 5 minutes. Transfer the lettuce to a serving plate.

Turn the heat to high and continue stirring until the ingredients emulsify and the juices turn a light-yellow color, about 3 minutes.

Spoon the bacon and its juices over the lettuce. Top with the toasted walnuts and serve immediately.

Pairs well with "Bloomdido" by Charlie Parker & Dizzy Gillespie

Summer Squash with Canned Sardines

Serves 4

Extra-virgin olive oil

1 golden zucchini, trimmed and cut
  lengthwise into ⅛-inch slabs

1 green zucchini, trimmed and cut
  lengthwise into ⅛-inch slabs

Leaves from 2 sprigs thyme

Salt

1 (3.75-ounce) can sardines in oil
  (I order King Oscar Brisling online)

Freshly squeezed juice of ½ lemon

1 tablespoon snipped chives
  (½-inch lengths) for garnish

¼ lemon, very thinly sliced

This small plate proves that very little time and effort can
sometimes have an incredible outcome—especially in the
summertime. The vegetables are just barely roasted, which
gives some sweetness and a little crunch but keeps the dish
light, fresh, and natural: perfect for a hot day. And, you can't
beat the ease (and taste!) of a can of sardines.

Preheat your oven to 375°F. Line a baking sheet with parchment paper
and brush the parchment lightly with olive oil.

Spread the zucchini in an even layer on the prepared baking sheet, and
lightly brush the zucchini with olive oil. Sprinkle with the thyme leaves
and a small pinch of salt. Bake for 10 minutes, then remove the pan from
your oven and set aside to cool to room temperature.

Layer the zucchini on your serving dish. Top with the sardines, a drizzle
of olive oil, and the lemon juice. Garnish with the chives and lemon slices.

Serve, or store covered in your refrigerator for up to 2 hours. Let the
squash come to room temperature before serving.

Pairs well with *"Big Bad Boy" by Alton Ellis*

Stewed Artichokes with Mozzarella

Serves 4 to 6

2 lemons

5 medium artichokes

2 tablespoons fresh marjoram leaves

1 teaspoon fresh thyme leaves
(from about 4 sprigs)

⅓ cup extra-virgin olive oil

1 medium carrot, peeled and diced
to ½ inch

1 medium white onion, diced to ½ inch

3 cloves garlic, thinly sliced

1 bay leaf

¾ cup dry white wine

2 tablespoons white wine vinegar

Salt

8 ounces fresh mozzarella, cut into
½-inch rounds

2 tablespoons fresh flat-leaf parsley
leaves, chopped

This salad utilizes some of my favorite ingredients (thyme, white wine, mozzarella) to accompany artichokes: the most magnificent of which can only truly be captured during springtime. Similar to an artichoke stew, this is my favorite way to cook the vegetable. Called barigoule, this traditional method of stewing artichokes in wine is also wonderful for serving them on their own, or perhaps with Mother-Sauce Mayo on the side (page 17).

Cut one of the lemons in half, and cut the other into four rounds. Fill a large bowl with cold water and squeeze one lemon half into the water. If you have gloves, put them on. If you don't, wash your hands and knives well after you've finished handling the artichokes—they leave a bitterness that sticks. Cut off and discard the artichokes' stems and remove their tough outer leaves, then use a bread knife to trim off the tops.

At this point, start working with one artichoke at a time—you want to dunk them in the lemon water as soon as possible to prevent browning. Trim off the artichoke's outer leaves so you're left with the white heart and delicate inner leaves. I use a sharp knife and work in a circular motion toward my thumb to trim the outer edge of the artichoke, but be careful for obvious reasons. Rub the other lemon half over the surface, then plunge it into the lemon water. Leave the trimmed artichoke in the lemon water while you trim the remaining artichokes. Finally, scoop out each choke, quarter it, and set aside on a paper towel to dry.

Very coarsely chop the marjoram and thyme leaves.

In a large pan on medium heat, stir together the olive oil, carrot, onion, and garlic. Cook for 2 minutes to lightly soften, then add the artichokes, marjoram, thyme, bay leaf, white wine, white wine vinegar, lemon rounds, and a healthy pinch of salt. Turn the heat to high. When the mixture comes to a simmer, turn the heat to low and cover the pan with the lid slightly ajar to allow steam to escape. Simmer until the artichokes have cooked through, 15 to 20 minutes. To test, poke an artichoke with a sharp knife to ensure you don't meet any resistance.

Pour everything onto your serving plate, remove the lemon rounds, and let the artichokes cool to room temperature. Top with the sliced mozzarella and parsley. Serve immediately, or cover and store in your refrigerator for up to 12 hours. Let it come to room temperature before serving.

Pairs well with *"Bald Headed Woman" by The Kinks*

Almond & Grape Gazpacho

Serves 4

8 ounces blanched sliced almonds, plus more, lightly toasted (see page 83) for garnish

1 clove garlic

2 slices white sandwich bread, crusts removed and middle torn into pieces (2 ounces total)

1 teaspoon salt

½ cup plus 1 teaspoon extra-virgin olive oil

1 tablespoon sherry vinegar

2 cups seedless grapes, halved

It helps to know: This recipe requires a blender.

This refreshing soup is my take on a white gazpacho, using ingredients you may already have in your pantry. The soup itself is creamy and bready, but the burst of fresh grapes gives an addicting contrast that makes a lovely first course or light lunch on a hot day. What's more, because it's served cold, it can be made the day before and kept covered in your refrigerator, ready to serve with ease. In fact, it gets even better overnight.

To soften the almonds and mellow out the garlic, cover them both with cold water in a small pot. Bring the pot to a simmer on high heat. Once the water begins to simmer, drain and return the almonds and garlic to the pot. Cover with cold water again and bring to a simmer on high heat. Once simmering, drain.

Transfer the softened almonds and garlic to a blender. Add the bread, salt, 3 cups cold water, and ¼ cup of the olive oil. Blend on high speed until everything is liquefied. Strain the soup through a fine-mesh strainer or cheesecloth over a large bowl, pushing hard with the back of a spoon to force the liquid through the paste that forms. Discard the paste.

Stir in the sherry vinegar and chill in your refrigerator for at least 45 minutes—or better yet, overnight.

Just before serving, toss the grapes with ½ teaspoon olive oil. Add 1 tablespoon olive oil to each of your four serving bowls. Ladle in the soup and garnish with plenty of grapes and toasted almonds.

Pairs well with "My Little Suede Shoes" by Charlie Parker and His Orchestra

Strawberry Gazpacho "Smoothie"

Serves 4 to 6

1¼ pounds strawberries, washed and hulled (see page 71)

1 small white onion, thinly sliced

1 red bell pepper, thinly sliced

1 cucumber, peeled, seeded, and thinly sliced

1 clove garlic, chopped

15 fresh tarragon or mint leaves

⅓ cup balsamic vinegar

½ cup extra-virgin olive oil, plus more for garnish

Salt

It helps to know: **This soup sits overnight and requires a blender.**

Strawberries in a gazpacho? If you think about it, there isn't much difference between a summer strawberry and a ripe tomato, especially when they're pureed.

This gazpacho has been a favorite recipe for years, not only at my restaurants but also in a pitcher in my refrigerator at home. I pour myself a glass and enjoy it as a smoothie in the morning, for a light lunch, or even as a first course at the Pink Palace in a bowl with a drizzle of olive oil.

Set the strawberries in a bowl large enough to hold all of the ingredients. With clean hands, crush the strawberries, squeezing them to release their juices. Have fun!

Add the onion, bell pepper, cucumber, garlic, tarragon, balsamic vinegar, and olive oil. Stir to mix well. Cover the bowl tightly with plastic wrap and chill in your refrigerator overnight.

The next day, puree the gazpacho in a blender. (I recommend blending in two batches so the blender doesn't overflow.) Season with a healthy pinch of salt to taste.

To serve, divide the gazpacho among six glasses or four bowls and top with a drizzle of olive oil.

Pairs well with *"Denis" by Blondie*

Onion & Brioche Soup with a Poached Egg & Manchego

4 tablespoons butter

1 clove garlic, chopped

2 pounds white onions, thinly sliced

Salt

3 cups Parmesan Stock (page 33), Chickpea Stock (page 34), Chicken Stock (page 32), or water

4 ounces brioche (or any seedless white bread, about the size of a softball), torn into bite-size pieces

½ teaspoon Dijon mustard

1 teaspoon sherry vinegar

4 to 8 ounces Manchego cheese

6 to 8 eggs (1 per serving), poached (see page 112)

1 tablespoon finely minced chives

Freshly ground black pepper

It helps to know: **This recipe requires a blender.**

A version of this soup was one of the first dishes on the menu when I opened Manresa more than fifteen years ago. It's still one of my favorite courses to this day, and it's easy enough to make at home.

Melt the butter in a large pot on low heat. Stir in the garlic, onions, and a pinch of salt and cook, stirring occasionally, until the onions are soft, about 25 minutes.

Add the stock and turn the heat to high. Once the soup is simmering, add the bread and turn the heat to low. Cover the pot with the lid slightly ajar to allow some steam to escape. Simmer for 20 minutes, stirring occasionally to prevent burning.

Carefully ladle the soup into a blender, filling it no more than half full (you may need to work in batches, depending on the size of your blender). Pulse slowly with the steam cap off until the soup is pureed and smooth, then strain through a fine-mesh strainer into a bowl. Stir in the Dijon mustard, sherry vinegar, and salt to taste.

Slice the cheese into ¼-inch-thick triangles, one slice per serving. Set the poached eggs in your serving bowls and top each with chives and a healthy pinch of pepper. Lay a Manchego slice on top of each egg. Ladle the hot soup over the cheese and serve.

Pairs well with *"Onions" by John Lee Hooker*

Two Chilled Soups

Serves 4 to 6

These refreshing summer soups showcase the pleasures of raw and cooked fruit. In both cases, the fruits are cut coarsely and heated until just the outside is cooked, leaving the flavor of the raw fruit in its center untouched. What's more, both soups can be made the day before and stored in your refrigerator until you're ready to serve. In fact, I'd even say that they taste better the following day.

Chilled Tomato & Garlic Soup

14 tomatoes (Early Girl or Roma preferred), peeled (see page 146)

½ cup extra-virgin olive oil

1 leek, trimmed, white part thinly sliced

Salt

5 cloves garlic, thinly sliced

⅓ cup balsamic vinegar

Garlicky Herbed Croutons (page 26) for garnish (optional)

Slice the tomatoes in half and squeeze them over the sink to discard their seeds.

In a large pan on medium heat, stir together the olive oil, leek, and a pinch of salt. Cook, stirring occasionally, until the leek has softened, 8 to 10 minutes.

Add the garlic and stir until soft but not brown, 1 to 2 minutes. Turn the heat to low and add the tomatoes and another pinch of salt. Use a wooden spoon to mash the tomatoes until they're broken but some larger pieces remain. Add the balsamic vinegar and stir to combine. Cover the pan and warm the soup to about 160°F. In other words, sipping temperature: cool enough to take small sips, but too hot to gulp; about 30 minutes.

Working in batches, transfer the soup to a blender and puree until smooth. Season with salt to taste, then set aside to cool to room temperature. Store in an airtight container in your refrigerator until nicely chilled.

Ladle the soup into six chilled glasses or four chilled bowls, top with a handful of croutons, and serve.

It helps to know: **These recipes require a blender.**

Pairs well with *"The Book"* by Eldridge Holmes

Chilled Melon Soup

1 large, very ripe (even overripe!) cantaloupe or honeydew melon, halved horizontally

Flaky sea salt

Sherry vinegar

½ cup butter

1 medium white onion, thinly sliced

Kosher salt

¼ cup blanched sliced almonds, lightly toasted (see page 83)

¼ cup almond oil

4 to 6 sprigs chervil (preferred) or tarragon

Set a strainer over a large bowl. Use a metal spoon to scrape the seeds and strings from the center of each melon half into the strainer. Press gently on the seeds using the back of the spoon to gather the juices in the bowl. (The juice from this part of the fruit is very high in pectin, a natural thickener found in ripe fruit, and is used to add texture to the soup.) Discard the seeds and strings and set the juice aside.

Use a sharp knife to peel the melon halves. Use a small melon baller or the knife to make ½ cup of teaspoon-size melon pieces. Place in a bowl and season with the flaky salt and sherry vinegar to taste. Set aside for 30 minutes.

Meanwhile, chop the remaining melon into golf ball–size pieces.

Drain and discard the excess liquid from the seasoned melon and set the melon "confit" aside.

In a pot over medium-low heat, combine the butter and onion and stir frequently until the butter has melted and the onion is soft and translucent, 25 to 30 minutes.

Add the large melon pieces and the reserved melon juice to the pot and cover with the lid slightly ajar to allow some steam to escape. Turn the heat to low and cook, stirring occasionally, until the melon has softened but not disintegrated and the soup has reached around 160°F. In other words, sipping temperature: cool enough to take small sips, but too hot to gulp; about 30 minutes.

Working in batches, transfer the soup to a blender and puree until smooth. Strain through a fine-mesh sieve (this is optional but will yield better overall texture). Season with kosher salt to taste, then set the soup aside to cool to room temperature. Store in an airtight container in your refrigerator until nicely chilled.

To serve, ladle the soup into six chilled glasses or four chilled bowls. Top with the toasted almonds and the melon "confit." Drizzle with the almond oil and garnish with a chervil sprig.

Pairs well with "We Got to Have Peace" by Curtis Mayfield

From left to right: Chilled Melon Soup; Chilled Tomato & Garlic Soup

Lettuce Vichyssoise

Serves 4

1 tablespoon butter

1 shallot, finely chopped

1 small white onion, finely chopped

1 clove garlic, finely chopped

Salt

1 cup heavy whipping cream

1 cup whole milk

3 hearts romaine

Crème fraîche for garnish

Garlicky Herbed Croutons (page 26)
  for garnish

Extra-virgin olive oil for drizzling

**It helps to know: This recipe
requires a blender.**

Vichyssoise is a traditional leek, potato, and cream soup that's served cold, making it both refreshing and rich. This is my take, in which the soup's predominant flavor comes from blanched romaine. This delicate vichyssoise is yet another example of the versatility of lettuce, and how it can be used for more than just salad. Feel free to make it the day before and store it in your refrigerator; just leave off the crème fraîche and croutons until the final moment.

In a medium pot on medium heat, melt the butter. Stir in the shallot, onion, garlic, and a pinch of salt. Cook, stirring occasionally, until the onion is soft but has no color, about 7 minutes.

Add the cream and milk and bring to a simmer. Once simmering, carefully pour everything into a blender.

Blanch the lettuce by bringing a large pot of water to a boil on high heat. Once boiling, add a pinch of salt. Use tongs to dunk one romaine heart at a time into the boiling water until it goes limp, about 30 seconds. Remove and set aside on a cutting board as you repeat with the remaining lettuce (don't pat it dry; you want it to retain some water when you blend).

Remove and discard the romaine heart's stems. Add a handful of lettuce to the blender and blend on high speed for 1 minute. Continue with the remaining lettuce, blending for 1 minute after each addition, until you've added all of the romaine.

Strain the soup through a fine-mesh strainer into a bowl to remove any leftover texture. Season with a healthy pinch of salt, then cover and chill in your refrigerator for at least 1 hour or up to 12 hours.

Just before serving, divide the soup among four bowls. Top each with a dollop of crème fraîche, a handful of croutons, and a drizzle of olive oil.

Pairs well with "Sound and Pressure" by Hopeton Lewis

ALL-DAY EGGS + 2 A.M. DINNERS

As a result of working in restaurants since I was 16, I've eaten a lot of dinners at two o'clock in the morning, and even more brunches at one o'clock in the afternoon. While the dishes in this chapter are perfect for coming home after a rowdy night out, they're also meant to be used for something slightly more meaningful: the practical.

When you come home hungry late at night with only cheese in your refrigerator and pasta in your pantry, turn to this chapter and my Cacio e Pepe (page 114). Better yet—turn to this chapter *before* you go out, ready yourself a Grilled Cheese (page 117), and leave it in your refrigerator to finish when you return.

I've included some egg dishes that will bring you back to life— eggs that are meant to be shared on a lazy day at one o'clock in the afternoon—like my Sweet & Savory Omelet Soufflés (page 108). I wrote this chapter to bestow some basic survival skills, and I can't think of anything more useful than knowing how to make the perfect egg. Learn how to cook eggs, and it will serve you (and others!) for the rest of your life.

These dishes require a stove or oven at most, and many, like the Pan Bagnat (page 118), don't even ask for heat (both for ease and safety purposes). I'll never make you plug anything in at 2 a.m. I promise you and your neighbors that no food processors or blenders will be involved. These are basic recipes that you can make at any hour of the day. Remember, no matter how tired you feel, food is essential to getting back on your feet. When you look back later, you'll thank yourself, and then you'll thank me.

Chorizo Frittata

Serves 8 to 10

12 ounces Yukon gold potatoes, peeled, halved, and cut into ¾-inch slices

Salt

8 ounces fresh chorizo

¼ cup plus 1 tablespoon extra-virgin olive oil

5 eggs

½ teaspoon espelette pepper or red pepper flakes

1 teaspoon freshly ground black pepper

Handful of small delicate greens

Classic Vinaigrette (page 24)

This frittata is easy and delicious for a casual weekend morning, especially to share among friends. Alternatively, you can leave off the greens and make it for a late weekend night (let's be honest, no one eats vegetables at 2 a.m.). But, if you do find yourself making this at a reasonable hour, the tangy salad cuts the spicy fattiness of the chorizo, and both are made infinitely more delicious by the addition of big chunks of creamy potato.

Preheat your oven to 375°F.

In a large pot, cover the potatoes with cold water. Bring to a simmer on high heat. Add a pinch of salt, turn down the heat to medium, and simmer, uncovered, until the potatoes have cooked through, about 15 minutes. Drain and set aside to cool to room temperature.

Meanwhile, in a small pan on medium heat, stir together the chorizo and 1 tablespoon of the olive oil. Use a wooden spoon to stir and break up the chorizo until it's cooked through, about 10 minutes. Set aside to cool to room temperature.

In a large bowl, gently whisk the eggs until just combined. Add the chorizo, potatoes, espelette pepper, 1 teaspoon salt, and the black pepper and stir to combine.

Heat the remaining ¼ cup olive oil in a medium oven-safe pan on high heat. When the oil begins to smoke, pour the egg mixture into the pan and cook, shaking the pan occasionally to prevent the eggs from sticking, until the eggs begin to crisp around the edges. Turn down the heat to medium and cook for 5 minutes, then put the pan in your oven.

Bake until the center no longer jiggles when you shake it, 7 to 10 minutes. Remove the pan from your oven and set aside for 10 minutes to allow the eggs to set.

Place your serving plate upside down on top of the pan. Flip the pan over so the crispy side of the frittata is facing up. Set the frittata aside to cool to room temperature.

Meanwhile, in a small bowl, dress the greens with a very small amount of the vinaigrette. To serve, slice the frittata like a pizza and scatter the salad over the top.

Pairs well with "Save Me" by Nina Simone

Crispy Fingerling Potatoes & Crispy Fried Eggs, Two Ways

These potatoes and eggs are great any time of day, but I especially love them for brunch. If you don't have time to make the potatoes, either one of the egg dishes would be good on its own or even better with a piece of crusty bread.

Crispy Fingerling Potatoes

1 pound fingerling potatoes

1 bay leaf

1 tablespoon kosher salt

Flaky sea salt

Sunflower oil

Fried eggs (recipes follow)

In a large pot, cover the potatoes with cold water. Turn the heat to low, add the bay leaf and kosher salt, and simmer, uncovered, until the potatoes are soft, about 30 minutes. To test for doneness, poke the largest potato with a knife to make sure you don't meet any resistance. Transfer the potatoes to a cutting board and let cool to room temperature.

Fold a large piece of parchment paper in half. Place one potato at a time in between the two sheets of parchment paper. Use the bottom of a heavy pot to carefully flatten the potato. Don't apply pressure too forcefully—you want it to remain in one piece. (This can also be done without parchment paper as long as the bottom of your pot is extra clean.) Season the potatoes generously with flaky sea salt.

In a large skillet on medium heat, heat enough oil to coat the bottom of the pan. Carefully set the potatoes in the pan and cook until the bottom sides are golden brown, about 5 minutes. Flip and cook until the other sides are golden brown, about 5 minutes more. Remove the potatoes from the pan and let drain on a paper towel.

Divide the potatoes among six plates and top each with the crispy fried egg of your choice.

Crispy Fried Eggs

WITH CAPERS, OLIVES & BREAD CRUMBS

1 teaspoon salt-packed capers

2 tablespoons extra-virgin olive oil

¼ cup dried bread crumbs

¼ cup water-packed pitted black olives, coarsely chopped

1 teaspoon fresh thyme leaves (from about 4 sprigs)

½ teaspoon red wine vinegar

Salt and freshly ground black pepper

Use a neutral, inexpensive oil for this technique: it's a bourgeois tragedy to use nice oil to fry an egg. I like this method because it gives you a crispy egg with a runny yolk, and, best of all, you never have to worry about it sticking to the pan. Make sure all of your cooking utensils are dry and the egg is at room temperature or the hot oil will sputter!

To serve with Capers, Olives & Bread Crumbs: Soak the capers covered with cold water in a small bowl for 10 minutes to remove their salt. Drain, coarsely chop, and set aside.

In a small pan on low heat, stir together the olive oil and bread crumbs. Toast, stirring often to prevent the bread crumbs from burning. When they

WITH GREEN GARLIC & GREEN ONIONS

1 cup sunflower oil

1 cup green onions, trimmed, white and tender green parts thinly sliced

1 cup green garlic, trimmed and thinly sliced

2 tablespoons soy sauce

1 tablespoon rice vinegar

1 tablespoon espelette pepper or hot paprika

Sunflower oil

6 eggs, at room temperature

begin to turn golden brown, add the olives, capers, and thyme. Continue to stir on low heat until warmed through and fragrant, about 1 minute.

Turn off the heat and deglaze the pan by stirring in the red wine vinegar. Add a pinch of salt and a twist of pepper. Serve over the eggs (see below) and potatoes, or store the mixture, covered, in your refrigerator for up to 3 days and serve it as a cold condiment.

To serve with Green Garlic & Green Onions: In a small pan on high heat, heat the sunflower oil.

Meanwhile, stir together the green onions and green garlic in a large bowl capable of holding high heat.

When the oil begins to smoke around the sides of the pan, carefully pour it over the allium mixture. The oil will cook the green onions and green garlic as it cools.

Stir in the soy sauce, rice vinegar, and espelette pepper and let the mixture cool to room temperature while you prepare the eggs. Serve over the eggs (see below) and potatoes, or store the mixture, covered, in your refrigerator for up to 3 days and serve it as a cold condiment.

To make the eggs: Set a small pan on high heat with enough sunflower oil to cover the bottom entirely (about ½ cup). Crack one egg into a small bowl or glass so you can get close enough to the pan to pour in the egg without splashing hot oil.

When the oil is smoking (make sure your fan is on high!), gently pour the egg into the pan. Wait a few seconds as the egg bubbles and sputters. Baste the egg by ladling the hot oil over the top with a large spoon. When the egg is outlined by a crispy, golden brown perimeter and its white is no longer runny, 2 to 3 minutes, remove it from the pan using a slotted spoon. Set the egg aside on a paper towel while you cook the remaining eggs, replenishing the oil as necessary.

Pairs well with "Papa Don't Take No Mess, Part I" by James Brown

⇢ From left to right: Green Garlic & Green Onions; Capers, Olives & Bread Crumbs

John Little Chicago's

STER
SES 97
London

CL 644

LP

Exclusive trade mark
of Columbia Records

MAHALIA JACKSON
The World's Greatest Gospel Singer

I'm Going to Live the Life I Sing
About in My Song

When I Wake Up in Glory

Jesus Met the Woman at the Well

Oh Lord, Is It I?

I Will Move On Up a Little Higher

When the Saints Go Marching In

Jesus

Out of the Depths

Walk Over God's Heaven

Keep Your Hand on the Plow

Didn't It Rain

with The Falls-Jones Ensemble

new songs for single
to get a

Savory & Sweet Omelet Soufflés

Serves 2

The following are considered soufflés because you whisk the egg whites, yielding fun, jiggly omelets that I like to make for a lazy brunch. Ignore your instincts to cook these until completely dry in the center. You want the omelets to be soft and almost flowing in the middle—just like a soufflé.

Savory

4 eggs, at room temperature

¼ cup finely grated Pecorino Romano, plus more for garnish

Freshly ground black pepper (I like a lot)

1 teaspoon salt

1 tablespoon finely minced chives, plus more for garnish

1 tablespoon butter

Divide the egg yolks and whites into separate bowls. Whisk the Pecorino Romano and black pepper into the egg yolks until the yolks have broken and combined with the cheese.

Using a hand whisk, beat the egg whites until they become frothy and begin to form soft peaks. In other words, when you lift the whisk up, the whites hold a peak for a second or two, but quickly melt back into themselves.

Just before you're ready to cook the omelet, stir the salt into the yolks. Resist any temptation to add the salt earlier or it will cook them.

Using a spoon, gently fold the egg yolk and cheese mixture into the egg whites and stir until incorporated—don't use a whisk or you risk overbeating the eggs! Stir in the chives.

In an 8- to 10-inch pan on medium-low heat, add the butter, and tilt the pan to coat the bottom as the butter melts. Once the butter begins to sizzle, pour in the egg mixture and let it sit without agitating the pan.

When the eggs begin to solidify on the outside but are still uncooked in the center, 2 to 3 minutes, cover the pan with a tight-fitting lid and let the mixture sit until the center is cooked but not dry, about 2 minutes more (I think of this as the omelet version of medium rare).

Remove the lid and carefully slide the omelet halfway out of the pan onto a plate so the bottom side is still facing down. Tilt the pan upside down to fold the second half onto itself to make an omelet.

Top with your desired amount of Pecorino Romano and chives. Slice in half and serve.

continued

Sweet

4 eggs, at room temperature

1 teaspoon granulated sugar

1 tablespoon honey

3 tablespoons crème fraîche

1 teaspoon salt

1 tablespoon butter

Jam of your choice (I like apricot)

Confectioners' sugar for dusting

Divide the egg yolks and whites into separate bowls. Gently stir the granulated sugar into the egg yolks until the yolks have broken and combined with the sugar.

In a separate bowl, stir together the honey and crème fraîche until combined. Set aside.

Using a hand whisk, beat the egg whites until they become frothy and begin to form soft peaks. In other words, when you lift the whisk up, the whites hold a peak for a second or two, but quickly melt back into themselves.

Just before you're ready to cook the omelet, stir the salt into the yolks. Resist any temptation to add the salt earlier or it will cook the yolks.

Using a spoon, gently fold the egg yolks into the egg whites until incorporated—don't use a whisk or you risk overbeating the eggs!

In an 8- to 10-inch pan on medium-low heat, add the butter, and tilt the pan to coat the bottom as the butter melts. Once the butter begins to sizzle, pour in the egg mixture and let it sit without agitating the pan.

When the eggs begin to solidify on the outside but are still uncooked in the center, 2 to 3 minutes, cover the pan with a tight-fitting lid and let the mixture sit until the center is cooked but not dry, about 2 minutes more (I think of this as the omelet version of medium rare).

Remove the lid and spread the crème fraîche and honey mixture over the top—or what will become the omelet's center. Carefully slide the omelet halfway out of the pan so the bottom side is still facing down. Tilt the pan upside down to fold the second half onto itself to make an omelet.

Top the omelet with jam, drizzle with any remaining crème fraîche and honey, and use a duster or fine-mesh strainer to sprinkle the top with a few healthy pinches of confectioners' sugar. Slice in half and serve.

Pairs well with *"There's a Light" by Shirley Ann Lee*

How to
Poach an Egg

There are a few ways to poach an egg, this method being my favorite. It's important to use a deep pot even though you're only poaching one egg at a time. The egg will hit the bottom and disassemble in a shallow pot; it needs to be deep enough for the egg to drop and reassemble around itself without hitting the bottom. Wait to add the salt until the very end, as adding salt to the water toughens the egg white.

1 teaspoon white wine or
   red wine vinegar

1 egg

Salt

Fill a medium to large pot three-quarters full with water. Add the vinegar and bring to a boil over high heat. Have a bowl of cold water ready.

Turn the heat to medium-low and wait until the water comes to a steady but gentle simmer. Crack an egg into a small bowl or glass.

Use a spoon to swirl the water, forming a whirlpool. As the water spins, pour the egg into the whirlpool's center. The swirling water will force the egg white to reassemble around the yolk.

Allow the egg to simmer for 3½ minutes. Use a slotted spoon to remove it from the water and plunge it into the bowl of cold water to stop it from cooking further.

After a few seconds, remove the egg from the cold water and place it on a paper towel to drain. Finish with a pinch of salt.

How to Hard-Boil an Egg

You can boil an egg in so many ways, but I like this method because it yields a hard-boiled egg with a perfect medium-cooked yolk. If your egg is pale yellow with a green perimeter, you've gone too far.

Add the desired number of eggs (without overcrowding the pot; they should all fit in a single layer at the bottom) to a large pot and cover with cold water. Set a bowl of cold water next to your stove.

Bring the water to a boil on high heat. Once boiling, turn down the heat to low to bring the water to a gentle simmer. Once simmering gently, set a timer for 6 minutes and 10 seconds.

Drain the eggs and immediately plunge them into the cold water to stop them from cooking further.

When it comes to peeling the eggs, I can't say I have a magic trick where the shell peels right off in one go. There are a few ways I've found that work well, such as shaking the egg in a tall glass of water with your palm over the top, or rolling the egg along the counter. Essentially, you want the eggshell to break all over the egg, rather than in one place.

Cacio e Pepe

Serves 4

Salt

1 tablespoon black peppercorns

1 pound bucatini, bigoli, or spaghetti

3 cups finely grated Pecorino Romano

1 cup finely grated
   Parmigiano-Reggiano

3 tablespoons extra-virgin olive oil

Since I always keep pasta and cheese on hand, this is my standard late-night meal enjoyed with a vibrant, fun red wine or a light beer. My advice regarding this classic dish is that cacio e pepe means "cheese and pepper"; in other words, pepper is a main ingredient. Don't take the pepper lightly—even the coarsest setting on your pepper mill will be too fine.

Bring a large pot of water to a boil on high heat. Once the water is boiling, add salt to taste.

Meanwhile, coarsely crush the peppercorns using a mortar and pestle. If you don't have a mortar and pestle, set the peppercorns on a sturdy cutting board. Using the bottom edge of a pot, forcefully press down and forward on the peppercorns until each corn is crushed. Don't be afraid to be aggressive. Both methods will yield peppercorns of all different sizes: a necessary quality of any good cacio e pepe.

Cook the pasta in the salted water according to the package directions to just before al dente. It should be slightly underdone, as the pasta will continue to cook after it's drained.

While the pasta is boiling, stir the cheeses together in a large bowl until combined. Ladle ½ cup of the boiling pasta water into the cheese and stir gently to form a paste.

Meanwhile, in a pot large enough to hold the pasta on low heat, stir together the olive oil and crushed peppercorns. Once fragrant, add 2 tablespoons of the boiling pasta water and stir to combine.

Reserve 1 cup of the pasta water and set aside. Drain the pasta and use tongs to gradually add the pasta to the pot with the olive oil and peppercorns. Stir vigorously while you add the pasta until it's coated in the oil and pepper.

Add the cheese paste and stir, keeping the heat on low, until the pasta is cooked to al dente and the sauce is creamy, 1 to 2 minutes. Add the reserved pasta water to thin out as necessary.

Add a pinch of salt to taste, but be conservative: the pasta will be salty from its cooking water and the natural saltiness of the cheeses. Serve.

Pairs well with "Nel Blu, Dipinto Di Blu" by Domenico Modugno

Grilled Cheese

Makes 1 sandwich

Butter, softened

2 (¾-inch-thick) slices country bread (sourdough preferred, or Manresa Bread's levain, if you can get it)

Dijon mustard

1 cup grated Gruyère cheese, plus 1 cup more if making cheese veil

2 small dill pickles, thinly sliced

1 ounce Taleggio, Robiola, or a similar soft, creamy cheese, cut to the size of 2 pats of butter

A grilled cheese sandwich is famously a quick and easy lunch, but it makes for an even better late-night snack. I've experimented with countless bread and cheese combinations, but the soft texture of melted Gruyère and Taleggio combined with sharp mustard and pickles, finished with a crispy cheese veil takes this sandwich to another level. I like to prepare it ahead of time and leave it in my refrigerator so it's ready to go after a long night. Use a well-seasoned cast-iron pan or a nonstick pan.

Liberally butter one side of each slice of bread. This will be the outside. Flip the bread over and spread a thin layer of Dijon on one half (or both, if you're a mustard person). On the other half, layer 1 cup of the Gruyère, the pickles, and the Taleggio.

Push the two halves together with the butter sides facing out to make a sandwich. Wrap the entire sandwich in plastic wrap and put in your refrigerator with something heavy on top (I use a heavy plate) for 30 minutes, or up to 12 hours, to compress.

When you're ready to serve, place the sandwich in a medium pan on medium heat. Place a heavy lid smaller than the pan directly on top of the sandwich. This will put pressure on the sandwich and the gathering steam will melt the cheese.

Once the bottom of the sandwich has browned, 5 to 7 minutes, use a wide spatula to flip it and place the lid back on top. When the second side is cooked to golden brown, 5 to 7 minutes more, remove from the pan and set aside.

From here, you can either eat the sandwich or make the cheese veil. The veil, passed down to me by my business partner Avery Ruzicka, is optional, but well worth the extra time.

Turn the heat to low and spread the remaining 1 cup of Gruyère directly onto the pan, just wide enough to cover the surface of the sandwich. The cheese will bubble up, melt, and start to turn brown like a pancake. When the cheese has begun to brown in the middle, set the sandwich in the center. Use a spatula to scrape the cheese up along the sides of the bread. Loosen the sandwich from the bottom of the pan, then flip it onto a plate so the cheese veil is on top. Slice the sandwich in half and serve.

Pairs well with "Night Life" by Ray Price

Pan Bagnat

Serves 2 to 4

2 anchovy fillets (salt-packed or
  oil-packed)

1 small clove garlic, minced

½ teaspoon Dijon mustard

1 teaspoon red wine vinegar

3 tablespoons extra-virgin olive oil

1 small cucumber, thinly sliced

1 large crusty round baguette
  or 2 to 4 ciabatta rolls

½ small red onion, thinly sliced

1 handful leaf lettuce, torn into
  bite-size pieces

4 small tomatoes (Early Girl
  or Roma preferred), cut into
  ¼- to ½-inch slices

Salt

5 ounces canned solid tuna packed
  in oil, drained

4 large basil leaves, torn into pieces

2 eggs, hard-boiled (see page 113),
  peeled, and sliced

½ cup pitted Niçoise olives, halved

This is one of my favorite sandwiches ever. I love the idea of softening day-old bread with the sandwich ingredients' juices. This is good for lunch, yes, but even better when it's waiting in your refrigerator at the end of a long day or night.

If your anchovies are salt-packed, soak them in water for 10 minutes to remove their salt. Drain.

Finely chop the anchovy fillets and place them in a large bowl. Whisk in the garlic, mustard, and vinegar to combine. Slowly whisk in the olive oil. Once combined, add the cucumber and stir to coat.

Cut the bread roll in half. Remove and discard the soft white center of each side so it resembles a hollow bowling ball.

Spread half of the cucumber mixture along the bottom slice of bread. Top with the red onion, lettuce, tomatoes, and a pinch of salt. Spread the tuna across the surface of the tomatoes. Top with the basil, eggs, and olives. Finish with the remaining cucumbers and a drizzle of the vinaigrette from the bowl.

At this point, your sandwich should resemble a precarious tower. Carefully cover the tower with the other half of the bread and wrap the entire sandwich in aluminum foil or plastic wrap. Put the wrapped sandwich in your refrigerator with a weight on top (I use a heavy pan) for 30 minutes. Flip, weight the other side, and let it sit in your refrigerator for another 30 minutes, or up to 12 hours.

To serve, cut the sandwich in halves or quarters and enjoy cold or at room temperature.

Pairs well with *"One for the Trouble" by Lack of Afro*

Pan con Tomate with Ham

Serves 6 to 8

1 loaf day-old sourdough, cut into
   1-inch slices

1 clove garlic, halved

3 large ripe heirloom tomatoes,
   halved

Extra-virgin olive oil

Flaky sea salt

About 4 ounces thinly sliced ham
   (jamón Serrano, prosciutto,
   or any cured pork)

This simple dish has become a staple of Pink Palace parties, and was the first recipe I wrote down when I started planning this cookbook. Every year since I first encountered Pan con Tomate in Spain, I've looked forward to the arrival of the first "best" tomatoes of summer so I can serve this toast. That said, *serve* may be an overstatement: I simply lay out the components and let my friends build their toasts as they like. Adding a paper-thin slice of ham may be gilding the lily, but I'll take my chances.

Preheat your oven to 400°F.

Arrange the bread slices in a single layer on a baking sheet and toast until they've firmed but haven't browned, about 2 minutes. Rub the garlic halves on one side of each slice, but be careful not to go overboard— I let my guests serve themselves, telling them "just a kiss" of garlic.

Rub the cut side of the tomato along the slices, allowing the juices to rehydrate them; discard the tomato. Top with a drizzle of olive oil, a healthy pinch of flaky sea salt, and thinly sliced ham. Eat with your hands, with your drink set somewhere nearby, no plate necessary.

Pairs well with "Beginning to See the Light" by The Velvet Underground

Herbed Goat Cheese & Chorizo Tartine with Honey

Serves 6 to 8

1 (10-ounce) goat cheese log

1¼ cups finely chopped fresh mixed
  herbs (such as chives, tarragon,
  parsley, and chervil)

Zest and juice from 1 lemon

½ cup heavy whipping cream

3 tablespoons extra-virgin olive oil,
  plus more for brushing

Salt and freshly ground black pepper

1 pound fresh chorizo

1 baguette, cut into ¼-inch slices

Honey for drizzling
  (I like chestnut honey)

Herbed goat cheese and spicy, salty chorizo on bread needs little introduction, but you may be wondering about the honey. While it may seem odd, the sweetness of the honey brings this toast together in a very fortunate way: sweet, spicy, savory, and addictive.

In a medium bowl, stir together the cheese, herbs, and lemon zest and juice until combined. Add the cream, olive oil, and a pinch each of salt and pepper. Cover and chill in your refrigerator for at least 1 hour to allow the herbs to infuse the cheese.

Meanwhile, in a medium pan on medium heat, add the chorizo and stir with a wooden spoon to break up the meat until it's cooked through, about 10 minutes. Set aside to cool to room temperature.

Preheat your oven or toaster oven to broil.

When you're ready to serve, very lightly brush the baguette slices with olive oil and toast them on a baking sheet in your oven or toaster oven until golden brown, about 1 minute per side. Spread the herbed goat cheese generously over each slice of toasted bread. Use a large spoon to scoop and pile on the chorizo. Finish with a drizzle of honey.

Serve immediately, with plenty of napkins on the side.

Pairs well with "El Bandido" by Georgie Fame & The Blue Flames

Mozzarella Crostini with Lemon & Tomato

Serves 4 to 6

About 8 ounces fresh mozzarella, cut into ½-inch rounds

Extra-virgin olive oil

Zest and juice of 1 Meyer lemon

1 loaf sourdough, cut into ¾-inch slices

1 clove garlic, halved

1 large heirloom tomato, halved

Flaky sea salt

This is a quick and easy toast for any time of day, from late at night to early morning. It's essentially the vegetarian version of the Pan con Tomate with Ham (page 120), using lemony, oily mozzarella cheese instead of pork. It's hard to beat ham, but this fresh, citrusy mozzarella toast comes pretty damn close.

Preheat your oven to 400°F.

Set the mozzarella slices in a small bowl. Top with a large glug of olive oil and the lemon zest and juice. Let the cheese marinate at room temperature for 15 minutes.

Meanwhile, arrange the bread slices in a single layer on a baking sheet and toast until they've firmed but haven't browned, about 2 minutes.

Rub the garlic on the sliced bread. Just a bit—you don't want the garlic to overpower the mozzarella and tomato.

Rub the cut sides of the tomato along the bread, allowing the juices to rehydrate it. Discard any remaining tomato and spread the mozzarella slices on top of the bread. Drizzle with the marinade and top with a pinch of flaky sea salt. Serve immediately.

Pairs well with "Rebel Rebel" *by David Bowie*

Toasted Baguette with Dark Chocolate, Olive Oil & Sea Salt

Serves 4

2 dark chocolate bars
(about 3 ounces each)

1 baguette, cut into 1-inch
slices and lightly toasted

Extra-virgin olive oil

Flaky sea salt

I once read that the great Catalan chef Ferran Adrià makes this simple toast for an afternoon snack. I've made it myself ever since to enjoy with a cup of coffee (see page 285) in the morning or as a late-night treat. I recommend using the best dark chocolate you can afford and not letting it melt too much in the oven; you want to maintain its shape. It's perfection.

Preheat your oven or toaster oven to broil. Line a baking sheet with aluminum foil.

Slice the chocolate bars into squares small enough to fit on top of the bread slices. Arrange the baguette slices in a single layer on the baking sheet. Top each slice with a piece of dark chocolate.

Broil until the chocolate is completely soft. The amount of time this takes will vary greatly depending on your chocolate—test the center with your finger to see if it has melted.

Once the chocolate has melted, finish with a drizzle of olive oil and a generous sprinkling of flaky salt over the top. Serve.

Pairs well with *"Worried about You" by The Rolling Stones*

PASTA + RICE

Sushi, in the most highly acclaimed restaurants in Japan, is not about fish. A spectacular piece of fish is important, sure, but sushi is meant to showcase the chef's mastery of the dish's main ingredient: rice. When done well, you can nearly taste each individual grain of rice in a piece of exceptional sushi. You can't tell if it's hot or cold: it's expertly timed to be served at the exact temperature of your body. The fish is the condiment.

I treat pasta with the same philosophy: the sauce is a condiment to the carbohydrate. And, when it comes to a chapter dedicated to rice and pasta, this philosophy is my opportunity to relinquish some responsibility. Cooking pasta and rice can be simple; my advice is to follow the instructions on the box. Pasta and rice, in the end, come down to timing. The different varieties may seem intimidating, but the best way to cook them is written directly on the package.

When it comes to my part—the condiment—these recipes are easy, satisfying crowd-pleasers. Everyone likes rice and pasta—and, to be honest, everyone especially likes pasta. In the face of pasta's popularity, rice holds its own with these dishes, even fighting for superiority. My jambalaya, for example, is an obvious favorite recipe for too many emotional reasons to put into words (though I've tried my best on page 150). Most of these recipes, like the Orecchiette & Broccoli alla Romana (page 133), are collected from "family meals" throughout the years, wherein an entire restaurant staff comes together before service to eat dinner prepared by the cooks. Some are more luxurious, like my Date-Night Risotto with Crab (page 147), and are meant to be shared with that special someone.

Though all of these dishes would make a tasty weeknight meal for one and provide leftovers throughout the week, like all of my recipes, they taste better with friends. I hope you use this chapter to make your own family meal, for the cherished people who distract you enough to leave the sauce simmering for too long (just add some water and stir; it'll be fine).

Bucatini with Canned Sardines & Capers

Serves 4

6 tablespoons salt-packed capers

4 tablespoon dried bread crumbs

½ cup extra-virgin olive oil

Salt

2 (3.75-ounce) cans sardines packed in olive oil, drained

1 clove garlic, finely chopped

2 tablespoons freshly squeezed lemon juice

Red pepper flakes

Espelette pepper or hot paprika

12 ounces bucatini, bigoli, or spaghetti

Fresh flat-leaf parsley leaves for garnish (optional)

I can wax poetic about canned sardines. It all started when I was living on a beginning cook's wage: a baguette, a big slab of butter, and a couple of sardines straight out of the can functioned as a meal on a regular basis. What started as a tartine of sustenance became an appreciation of the sardine's cultural significance, its health benefits, and the ease of having them on hand at all times in my pantry. To me, sardines and butter is an eye-roll-to-the-back-of-the-head flavor. I won't get into the cult of vintage sardines, and the connoisseurs who age certain brands like wine—often for years, to add a complexity of flavor. I'll just say this: they're a delicacy in a $2.00 can.

In a fine-mesh strainer, rinse the capers with cold water, then soak them covered with cold water in a small bowl for 10 minutes to remove their salt. Drain and set aside.

Meanwhile, in a medium pan on low heat, fry the bread crumbs with ¼ cup of the olive oil, stirring frequently until they turn golden brown, 5 to 7 minutes. Drain using a fine-mesh strainer and spread onto a paper towel. Set aside.

Bring a large pot of water to a boil on high heat. Once boiling, add salt to taste.

In a large bowl, combine the sardines, capers, garlic, the remaining ¼ cup olive oil, the lemon juice, and a pinch each of red pepper flakes, espelette pepper, and salt. Stir using a fork to coarsely break up the sardines.

Add the bucatini to the salted water and cook to al dente, according to the package instructions.

While the pasta is cooking, add 3 tablespoons of the pasta water to the sardine mixture and stir to combine.

Drain the pasta and stir it into the bowl with the sardine mixture. Stir aggressively to finish breaking up the sardines and coat the pasta evenly. The pasta's starch will give the sauce a creamy consistency.

Divide among four bowls. Top with the toasted bread crumbs and parsley and serve immediately.

Pairs well with "Too Much Time" by Captain Beefheart and His Magic Band

Orecchiette & Broccoli alla Romana

Serves 4 to 6

2 ounces anchovies (oil-packed or salt-packed)

1 tablespoon salt-packed capers

1 head broccoli

¼ cup extra-virgin olive oil

3 cloves garlic, finely chopped

Salt

Freshly ground black pepper

Red pepper flakes

1 pound orecchiette

About ½ cup grated Pecorino Romano

Typically the objective when cooking broccoli is to ensure that the florets remain intact and retain their vibrant green color. I love this recipe because it breaks those rules: both the broccoli head and stems are roughly chopped and slowly simmered until they turn an olive green. In many ways it reminds me of how green beans are often cooked in the Deep South: thrown in a pot with bacon and cooked until they're nearly unrecognizable and super-delicious. This slow-cooked broccoli combined with red pepper flakes, garlic, and anchovies—three very strong flavors—make this vegetable shine.

In a fine-mesh strainer, rinse the anchovies and capers with cold water, then soak them covered with cold water in a small bowl for 10 minutes to remove their salt. Drain, coarsely chop, and set aside.

Meanwhile, to prepare the broccoli, cut off and peel the thick stems. Coarsely chop both the heads and the stems.

In a large pot on medium heat, combine the broccoli, olive oil, garlic, and a generous pinch of salt. Cover the pot with the lid slightly ajar to allow steam to escape. Cook, stirring occasionally, until the broccoli is soft, 10 to 12 minutes.

When the broccoli is completely soft, turn the heat to low and add ½ cup water, the anchovies, capers, and a healthy pinch each of salt, black pepper, and red pepper flakes to the pot. Cook until the broccoli has broken down to a sauce and turned an olive green, about 20 minutes more.

Bring a large pot of water to a boil on high heat. Once boiling, add salt to taste.

Add the pasta and follow the instructions on the package to cook until just before al dente, setting aside a cup of the pasta water before draining.

Ladle 2 tablespoons of the pasta water into the pot with the broccoli and stir, keeping the heat on medium.

Drain the pasta and stir it directly into the pot with the broccoli. Add the reserved pasta water to thin out as necessary. Top with the Pecorino Romano and serve immediately.

Pairs well with *"La Donna Riccia" by Domenico Modugno*

Lamb Bolognese with Tagliatelle

Serves 6 to 8

3 tablespoons sunflower oil

1 large carrot, peeled and diced

1 large white onion, diced

2 ribs celery, diced

Salt

1 clove garlic, finely chopped

8 ounces ground lamb

8 ounces ground pork

1 cup whole milk

1 cup dry white wine

1 teaspoon freshly ground
    black pepper, plus more to taste

2 (28-ounce) cans whole tomatoes
    (I use San Marzano)

1 whole nutmeg (optional)

2 pounds tagliatelle

Freshly grated Parmigiano-Reggiano
    for serving

It helps to know: Give yourself some extra time with this one. It's simple to make, but it sits on the stove (with minimal stirring involved) for 3 to 3½ hours.

This Bolognese uses the fat of the pork to balance the leanness of the lamb while keeping the lamb's distinct flavor. I love the sound of this sauce cooking: the light pop a single bubble of steam makes as it escapes every 15 seconds or so. It's the sound of a low simmer; the sound of an incredibly delicious slow-cooked sauce sitting on the stove. Be sure to use a large pot, as this recipe makes more than you'll likely need, but it freezes exceptionally well stored in an airtight container for up to 1 month.

Heat the oil in a large pot over medium heat. Add the carrot, onion, celery, and a pinch of salt and cook, stirring occasionally, for 5 minutes. Add the garlic and continue to cook until the vegetables have softened, about 5 minutes more.

Add the lamb and pork and use a wooden spoon to break up the meat into smaller pieces. Continue to stir and break up the meat until it no longer looks raw, about 15 minutes.

Add the milk to deglaze (see page 196) and turn the heat to high. Cook, stirring occasionally, until the milk evaporates, about 5 minutes. Add the white wine and pepper and continue stirring occasionally until the wine has evaporated, about 5 minutes.

Pour the cans of tomatoes into a large bowl. Squeeze the tomato chunks with your hands to break them apart. Add the crushed tomatoes and their juices to the pot and stir to combine. Turn the heat to low and cover your pot with the lid slightly ajar to allow steam to escape. Gently simmer until the sauce thickens considerably, 3 to 3½ hours, lifting the lid occasionally to stir.

Taste and adjust the salt and pepper levels to your liking. Grate in the nutmeg using a spice grater or Microplane until you've used about one-quarter of the nutmeg. Stir to combine. I love this addition, but ground nutmeg (or sawdust, as I like to call it) is not an acceptable substitute. If you don't have a whole nutmeg to freshly grate, just leave it out.

Bring a large pot of water to a boil on high heat. Once boiling, add salt to taste. Add the tagliatelle and follow the instructions on the package to cook to al dente.

Divide the pasta among bowls or plates. Top with the Bolognese and grated Parmigiano-Reggiano.

Pairs well with "Don't Take Your Guns to Town" by Johnny Cash

Spaghetti "Soffritto"

Serves 4

4 pounds tomatoes (Early Girl or Roma preferred)

2 cups extra-virgin olive oil

1 teaspoon sugar

Salt

1 bay leaf

4 medium white onions, finely diced

2 teaspoons smoked paprika

2 cloves garlic, finely chopped

1 pound spaghetti

Freshly grated Parmigiano-Reggiano for serving

Slowly cooked, caramelized onions with fresh summer tomatoes and a touch of smoked pimentón are the classic flavors of a Spanish-style sofrito. It was an easy next step to treat the combination as a red sauce for pasta, hence this Spaghetti "Soffritto." Though this sauce is delicious on day one, it makes for even better leftovers. Consider doubling the recipe as it will keep in your refrigerator, covered in a layer of olive oil, for up to 2 weeks.

Cut the tomatoes in half horizontally. Using the large side of a box grater, grate the cut side of each tomato into a large bowl, discarding the skins.

In a large pot on low heat, combine the olive oil, sugar, 1 teaspoon salt, the bay leaf, and the onions, and cook, stirring occasionally, until the onions start to lightly brown, about 40 minutes.

Add the smoked paprika and garlic and stir to combine. Stir in the tomatoes and continue simmering until the sauce reduces and the oil separates, about 25 minutes.

Meanwhile, bring a large pot of water to a boil on high heat. Once boiling, add salt to taste. Add the spaghetti and follow the instructions on the package to cook to al dente, setting aside 1 cup of the pasta water.

Add the spaghetti to the sauce along with 2 tablespoons of the pasta water. Stir to coat, adding more pasta water to thin out the sauce if necessary.

To serve, divide the pasta among four bowls or plates and top with Parmigiano-Reggiano to taste.

Pairs well with "El Último Trago" by Chavela Vargas

Penne with a Walnut Sauce

Serves 6

About 1¼ cups raw walnuts, coarsely chopped

1 clove garlic, crushed

2 tablespoons dried bread crumbs

5 ounces (about ¾ cup) whole milk ricotta

5 tablespoons whole milk

Dried marjoram (optional)

5 tablespoons extra-virgin olive oil

¼ cup finely grated Parmigiano-Reggiano

Kosher salt and freshly ground black pepper

1 pound penne

Fresh or lightly fried marjoram leaves for garnish (optional)

It helps to know: **This recipe requires a food processor or blender.**

This white pesto is creamy and cheesy and nutty, and though inexpensive to make, it feels rather luxurious nonetheless. Be careful not to overprocess this; it should have some texture like a traditional pesto. This recipe makes more pesto than you'll probably use for a box of pasta, but it keeps for up to 2 days, covered, in your refrigerator. And, like the other takes on pesto in this book (see pages 22 and 170), this is delicious on toast, as a dip, or in any number of the dishes in which you'd use a traditional pesto.

In a food processor or blender, pulse together the walnuts, garlic, bread crumbs, ricotta, milk, and a pinch of marjoram. On low speed, slowly drizzle in the olive oil, 1 tablespoon at a time, until incorporated. Gently pulse in the Parmigiano-Reggiano and season with salt and pepper to taste.

Bring a large pot of water to a boil. Once boiling, add salt to taste. Add the penne and cook according to the package instructions until al dente. Set aside 1 cup of the pasta water.

Drain the penne and transfer it to a large bowl. Slowly add the pesto and stir until the pasta is well coated, using pasta water to thin out the sauce as necessary. You likely won't use all of the pesto: a small amount goes a long way.

Divide among six bowls or plates, top with the marjoram leaves, and serve.

Pairs well with "*I'm on Fire*" *by Dwight Twilley Band*

Pasta with Pesto & Avocado

Serves 4

Salt

2 tablespoons Seven-Ingredient Pesto
(page 22)

1 pound trofie, bucatini, tagliatelle,
or spaghetti

1 ripe avocado, peeled, seeded,
and cubed to about ½ inch

Freshly grated Parmigiano-Reggiano
for serving (optional)

In many ways, the Mediterranean coasts of France and Italy remind me of my home in California. As a result, I've given my California take on a Ligurian pasta a lot of thought. In Europe, in the small towns facing the sea, chefs add potatoes and green beans to stretch their pasta as a nod to their tradition of frugality. In California, I add avocado.

Bring a large pot of water to a boil on high heat. Once the water is boiling, add salt to taste.

Scoop the pesto into a bowl large enough to hold the pasta.

Add the trofie to the pot and follow the instructions on the package to cook to al dente. Just before it's finished cooking, ladle ¼ cup of the pasta water into the pesto and stir to thin. Don't worry if the pesto looks too thin: the sauce will thicken from the starch of the pasta. Reserve an additional 1 cup of pasta water.

Drain the pasta and stir it into the pesto, adding the reserved pasta water, if necessary. When the pasta is coated, gently stir in the avocado. Finish with a pinch of salt to taste.

Divide among four bowls or plates, top each with a sprinkle of cheese, and serve immediately.

Pairs well with *"The Look of Love" by Dusty Springfield*

Linguine with Clams & Shrimp

Serves 4

1 pound Manila or littleneck clams, in the shell

Salt

½ cup extra-virgin olive oil

1 white onion, chopped

2 cloves garlic, finely chopped

12 ounces extra jumbo (16/20) shrimp, peeled

½ cup dry white wine

1 pound linguine

½ cup fresh flat-leaf parsley leaves, chopped

This dish is a classic linguine with clams with one small upgrade: one of my favorite crustaceans. Serve it in the summer months, with a bowl in the middle of the table for the shells, and a glass of chilled white wine or rosé alongside each plate.

Rinse the clams thoroughly in cold water, then soak them in cold water for 30 minutes. Rinse thoroughly once more to remove any remaining sand, then drain and set aside, discarding any clams that have opened.

Bring a large pot of water to a boil on high heat. Once boiling, add salt to taste.

Meanwhile, in a large pot on medium heat, stir together the olive oil, onion, and a pinch of salt. Cook until the onion has softened but hasn't taken on any color, about 7 minutes. Add the garlic and stir until it's soft but hasn't taken on any color, 1 to 2 minutes.

Add the shrimp and stir to combine. Turn the heat to high and add the clams and white wine. Cover the pot with a tight-fitting lid and steam until the clams open and release their juices, about 2½ minutes. Strain the pot over a bowl to reserve the juices. Return the juices to the pot and reduce over high heat until the liquid foams and thickens, about 3 minutes.

Meanwhile, add the linguine to the pot of boiling water and cook to al dente according to the package instructions.

Drain the pasta through a colander and add it along with the shellfish, onions, garlic, and parsley to the reduced juices. Stir until the pasta has absorbed some of the liquid and is nicely coated in the sauce.

Divide the pasta among four plates or bowls and serve immediately.

Pairs well with "Soul Sauce" by Cal Tjader

Ricotta Gnocchi with a Simple Tomato Sauce

Serves 6 to 8

1¾ pounds tomatoes (Early Girl or Roma preferred), peeled (see page 146)

½ cup extra-virgin olive oil

2 medium shallots, finely diced

1 bay leaf

Salt and freshly ground black pepper

Sugar

2 sprigs basil

About 1 cup all-purpose flour

12 ounces whole milk ricotta

Shaved Pecorino Romano for garnish

I was helping a friend open his restaurant when he made this tomato sauce for his staff dinner. I loved how fresh it tasted, but more than that, I was impressed by how quickly it came together. While gnocchi may seem time-consuming or laborious, this version, which is made by simply rolling ricotta in flour, is as simple as the sauce. Together, they make an extravagant-feeling meal that gives the illusion of time and effort while secretly being quick and easy to make.

Cut the tomatoes in half and squeeze their seeds over the sink to discard. Put the remaining flesh into your blender, and blend on low speed until a smooth puree forms.

In a large pot on low heat, stir together the olive oil and shallots until the shallots have softened without browning, about 4 minutes. Shallots burn easily—be sure to keep the heat low and stir frequently.

Add the tomato puree, the bay leaf, and a healthy pinch each of salt and pepper. Turn the heat to medium and bring the sauce to a simmer. Add a small pinch of sugar and stir to combine. Once the sauce begins to simmer, turn the heat to low and cook, stirring occasionally, for 12 minutes.

Remove the pot from the heat, stir in the basil, and set aside to cool to room temperature. Once cool, remove the basil and discard.

Meanwhile, prepare the gnocchi. On a large cutting board, pile the flour next to the ricotta. Top the ricotta with 1 teaspoon black pepper and gently roll it into the flour, pushing the ricotta forward and flipping it until the ricotta and flour combine to form a consistency similar to wet dough. The amount of flour you use will depend on your ricotta, but it should be around 1 cup.

Sprinkle a handful of flour across a clean cutting board to prevent the cheese from sticking. With plenty of flour on your hands, form the dough into a ball and use your palm to flatten out the top so the dough is about 1 inch thick.

Cut the flattened dough into 1-inch-wide slices that resemble breadsticks. Roll out each slice into a log about ¾ inch in diameter, then cut each log into a ¾-inch "pillow."

It helps to know: **This tomato sauce requires a blender.**

continued

continued

Dip the prongs of a fork into the flour and then onto the top of each gnocchi pillow. Applying gentle pressure, pull the fork toward you until the ball spirals to resemble a seashell, about one half-full turn. Do this one at a time, setting aside the finished gnocchi on a paper towel, spaced without touching to prevent them from sticking to each other.

Just before serving, bring a large pot of water to a boil on high heat. Once boiling, add salt to taste.

Reheat the tomato sauce over low heat. Taste and adjust the salt level to your liking.

Cook the gnocchi for 1 minute in the boiling water. Remove carefully using a slotted spoon and place on your serving dish. Top with the tomato sauce and Pecorino Romano and serve immediately.

Pairs well with *"Ali Baba" by John Holt*

HOW TO PEEL TOMATOES

Bring a large pot of water to a boil over high heat, and place a bowl of cold water next to your stove.

Use a small knife to cut a shallow circle around the top of each tomato, removing its stem. Flip the tomato upside down and slice a very shallow X on its bottom, just piercing the skin. Though this step isn't totally necessary, it will make peeling slightly easier.

Use a spoon to lower each tomato into the pot of boiling water for 15 seconds, then immediately plunge it into the cold water to stop it from cooking further.

Remove the tomato from the cold water. Use your thumb and the small knife against the four small triangles you created with the X cut, and peel the skin downward to remove.

Date-Night Risotto with Crab

Serves 2 to 4

3½ cups Chickpea Stock (page 34), Chicken Stock (page 32), or store-bought low-sodium vegetable stock

¼ cup butter

1 tablespoon extra-virgin olive oil

1 medium white onion, finely chopped

1¾ cups Arborio or Carnaroli short-grain rice (I use Carnaroli)

½ cup dry white wine

Salt

8 ounces lump crabmeat

1 heaping tablespoon mascarpone cheese

Nothing says date night like a risotto, and I reserve this one in particular for my favorite guest at the Pink Palace. Why is this my date-night dish, you ask? Because of its rich, creamy texture and it uses only two pots. It requires stirring frequently, but you can also have a glass of wine and engage in charming conversation while you look your best standing by the stove. I especially love this dish in the summertime with blanched fava beans or asparagus. Stir them in just before serving to make this risotto extra special.

Before I leave you to it—the mistake everyone makes with risotto, even in restaurant kitchens, is that they overcook the rice. In fact, I would rather eat an undercooked risotto than a bowl of mush. Don't overcook it and be sure to eat it right away.

In a small pot on low heat, bring the stock to a simmer.

Meanwhile, in a large pot on medium-low heat, stir together the butter and olive oil. When the butter has melted and combined with the oil, add the onion and continue stirring until the onion is soft but hasn't taken on any color, about 7 minutes.

Add the rice and turn the heat to medium. Continue stirring to coat the rice in the oil and lightly toast the grains until they begin to crackle but don't take on any color, about 2 minutes. Add the white wine and continue stirring until the wine has evaporated and the rice begins to crackle again.

Add enough of the simmering stock to cover the rice, about ½ cup. Add a healthy pinch of salt and gently stir frequently until the stock has evaporated. Continue adding the stock in ½-cup increments along with a pinch of salt. Gently stir as you add the stock, allowing the rice to absorb the liquid, until you've added all the stock and the rice is wet and creamy, 20 to 22 minutes total. Taste the rice and add more salt, if necessary. The final result should be toothsome but not raw and have the texture of a porridge.

Stir in the crab and mascarpone and serve immediately.

Pairs well with *"To Be Alone with You" by Bob Dylan*

Rice Cremoso with Clams

Serves 6 to 8

2 pounds Manila or littleneck clams, in the shell

4 cups fish stock, Chicken Stock (page 32), or Chickpea Stock (page 34)

1 white onion, diced

1 clove garlic, finely chopped

¼ cup extra-virgin olive oil

Salt

8 ounces spicy Italian sausage, cut into 1-inch rounds

1 cup short-grain white rice

½ cup dry white wine

Freshly squeezed lemon juice

1 tablespoon fresh flat-leaf parsley, chopped

Clams and sausage infuse rice with tons of assertive flavor in this super Spanish-style rice dish, but what I adore even more than the resulting explosive taste is the unique texture. Somewhere between a porridge and a risotto and a soup, this cremoso (Spanish for "creamy") is warm and homey and comforting. It's lucky this dish is so easy to make, as you'll find yourself craving it on a regular basis, especially on cold winter nights.

Rinse the clams thoroughly in cold water, then soak them in cold water for 30 minutes. Rinse thoroughly once more to remove any remaining sand, then drain and set aside, discarding any clams that have opened.

In a medium pot on high heat, bring ½ cup of the stock to a boil. Once boiling, add the clams and cover the pot. Steam the clams, shaking the pot vigorously every 30 seconds with the lid on, until the clams have opened, about 2½ minutes. Remove the pot from the heat and set aside, uncovered.

In a large pot on medium heat, bring the remaining 3½ cups stock to a simmer.

Meanwhile, in a large pan on low heat, stir together the onion, garlic, and olive oil. Add a pinch of salt and cook until the onion is soft but has no color, about 10 minutes.

Add the sausage and cook to medium rare, about 5 minutes. Add the rice and turn the heat to medium. When the rice starts to sizzle, add the wine and stir to combine. Simmer until the wine has evaporated, about 5 minutes.

Ladle 1 cup of the simmering fish stock into the rice mixture. Simmer for 2 minutes, stirring occasionally. Add a pinch of salt and another cup of fish stock. Continue adding the stock, 1 cup at a time, every 2 minutes until you've added all of the simmering stock. The final result will yield cooked rice with a soupy consistency.

Stir in the cooked clams, lemon juice to taste, and the parsley. Serve.

Pairs well with "This Town" by Frank Sinatra

A Love Letter
to New Orleans

I've been accused of being a "California chef." My affinity for surfing, my infatuation with the fresh produce, and my fascination with the landscape where the mountains meet the sea have made the Golden State an easy place to settle. But while I adore all of the above enough to make California my home for the past twenty-five years, my heart still lives in New Orleans: In the condensation that forms on the cold glass of an afternoon porch drink. In the sweaty bars at three o'clock in the morning during the weekend of Jazzfest. In a second line behind a marching brass band. In choking on powdered sugar from inhaling beignets too quickly. In the piles of crayfish, crab, and shrimp stacked on top of newspapers with a trash can nearby for the remnants. In people's willingness to strike up a conversation with a stranger, free from judgment or expectations, and full of curiosity.

I owe everything I have to New Orleans and its people. It was when I moved there as a teenager that I truly discovered food and the culture that surrounds it. It was there that I first worked in a kitchen. And where I first learned to cook. The city forever altered the trajectory of my life. I haven't lived there for a long time, but to this day, with no waves to surf or coastline to admire, it still feels like home.

You'll find small pieces of NOLA scattered throughout this book, mostly in the drinks section (if you don't know by now, the people of New Orleans know how to have a good time). If I had to pick a standout, though, my jambalaya recipe is my personal love letter to the city.

Jambalaya, New Orleans Style

Serves 8

¼ cup sunflower oil

3 cups diced white onions
(about 2 large onions)

1 cup diced celery (about 2 ribs)

2 cups diced green bell peppers
(about 2 large peppers)

1 bay leaf

4 teaspoons freshly ground
black pepper

1 teaspoon garlic powder (optional)

1 teaspoon onion powder (optional)

Salt

1 cup trimmed and thinly sliced
green onions, white and
tender green parts only

2 cups (about 1 pound) sliced
andouille sausage (½-inch rounds)

2 cups long-grain white rice

2½ cups Chicken Stock (page 32)
or store-bought low-sodium
chicken stock

1 tablespoon Worcestershire sauce

1 teaspoon cayenne

1 pound extra jumbo (16/20) shrimp in
shells, rinsed well with cold water

24 shucked oysters in their water

This is the perfect Pink Palace dish: it's not fancy or extravagant, it's not trying to impress anyone, it's just really, really good. But what I love even more about jambalaya is that there's no such thing as making it for two people. Gather your friends (and their friends), ask them to bring beer, and eat it at your table together, or while you're all standing around your kitchen, or sitting out on the porch: there's really no wrong way to share a jambalaya.

Preheat your oven to 375°F.

In a large oven-safe pot on high heat, heat the sunflower oil until it's just starting to smoke. Add the white onions, celery, and bell peppers ("the holy trinity") and cook, stirring often, until the vegetables start to soften, about 2 minutes. Add the bay leaf, black pepper, garlic powder, onion powder, and a healthy pinch of salt and continue to cook until the vegetables caramelize and turn brown, 12 to 15 minutes. You'll see brown bits start to stick to the bottom of your pot—this is the fond (see page 196), in other words, the best part.

Add the green onions and continue to stir until they wilt, about 1 minute. Add the sausage and continue to cook until the fat renders and the sausage gets crispy, about 2 minutes. Stir in the rice and a generous pinch of salt.

Add the chicken stock and Worcestershire sauce and scrape up the brown bits that have formed. Turn down the heat to low. Stir in the cayenne and wait as the pot comes to a simmer. Add a pinch of salt, taste, and add more, if necessary.

Turn up the heat to high, and when boiling, add the shrimp and the oysters and their water. The shellfish will be slightly overcooked, but it adds tremendous amounts of flavor to the rice—a compromise I can live with.

Cover the pot with a tight-fitting lid and transfer it to your oven for 14 minutes. Remove the pot from your oven and resist the temptation to peek. Let it sit, covered, for 10 minutes.

Serve immediately or store in your refrigerator, covered, for up to 12 hours. Simply let it come to room temperature before serving.

Pairs well with "Where There's Smoke There's Fire" by Buckwheat Zydeco

Paella

SOFRITO

4 pounds tomatoes (Early Girl or Roma preferred)

2 cups extra-virgin olive oil

1 teaspoon sugar

1 teaspoon salt

1 bay leaf

4 medium white onions, finely diced

2 teaspoons smoked paprika

2 cloves garlic, finely chopped

RICE AND SHRIMP

1 pound extra jumbo (16/20) shrimp in shells, rinsed well with cold water

Salt

¼ cup extra-virgin olive oil

2 cloves garlic, finely chopped

4 cups fish stock, Chicken Stock (page 32), or Chickpea Stock (page 34)

1 teaspoon saffron threads, lightly toasted and crushed

2 cups Bomba rice

It helps to know: **This recipe requires a 12-inch or larger paella pan.**

The truth is, this recipe isn't a result of working in Spain, or any romantic story from my past. I just really, really like rice and shellfish, so I've made a lot of paella. The base for this recipe is the same as the sauce for the Spaghetti "Soffritto" (page 137), so consider doubling it and having extra pasta sauce to last you throughout the week.

To make the sofrito, cut the tomatoes in half horizontally. Using the large side of a box grater, grate the cut side of each tomato into a large bowl, discarding the skins.

In a large pot on low heat, stir together the olive oil, sugar, salt, bay leaf, and onions and sauté until the onions start to lightly brown, about 40 minutes.

Add the smoked paprika and garlic and stir to combine. Stir in the tomatoes and simmer until the sauce reduces and the oil separates, about 25 minutes. Set aside.

To make the rice and shrimp, in a medium bowl, toss the shrimp with a pinch of salt.

Heat the olive oil in your paella pan on medium heat. When the oil is hot, add the shrimp in one layer. Let them sit for 1 minute to give them a little color, then use tongs to flip and cook for 1 minute more. Be careful not to overcook the shrimp here—you'll need them to remain raw so their juices later season the rice. Remove the shrimp from the pan and set aside.

Pour the sofrito into the paella pan with the heat still on medium. Add the garlic and cook, stirring frequently, until it softens but doesn't take on any color, about 5 minutes. Stir in the fish stock, 1 tablespoon salt, and the saffron and bring to a simmer.

Once simmering, add the rice and stir to combine. Pour in any juices that formed at the bottom of the bowl of shrimp and stir to combine. Add the shrimp in one single layer. Let everything sit without stirring until a crust forms on the bottom and the rice cooks through, 14 to 16 minutes.

To serve, scoop the top layer of rice and shrimp into bowls, leaving the blackened crust in the pan.

Pairs well with "Miles Runs the Voodoo Down" by Miles Davis

FISH + SHELLFISH

I disappear every so often to sleep on a sailboat. I'm lucky to have a job where I often get to be a tourist: stealing moments to visit the unforgettable restaurants and local markets and art museums. I'm beyond grateful for these experiences, but they're not my break. The older I get, the better I understand that my mental, physical, and emotional health depend on the sun and the sea. So, for a week of each year, I go as far out to the middle of the ocean as a chartered sailboat captain will take me, far enough (at a minimum) that checking my email is impossible. I wake up to the sun on my face and spend the afternoon catching a fish for dinner. I may be thousands of miles from home, but it doesn't feel like I'm traveling. It's my time to recharge.

My fascination with the ocean started as a young boy spending summers on the Jersey Shore with my family. It was there that I had my first food epiphany. I was at a family barbecue when my uncle gave me a steamed clam. I was never the same. Having been raised on a typical Pennsylvania diet (think meat, potatoes, pot pies, and corn), I found steamed shellfish to be wonderfully exotic: sweet and simple and chewy and ineffably fresh. It tasted like the ocean, like my own piece of the endless blue expanse I had spent the entire summer admiring from afar.

The ocean has continued to nurture me in tangible and intangible ways ever since. I've devoted a huge portion of my life to worshiping it in every way possible, from surfing its waves to spending too many hours gutting and shucking and braising and poaching and baking and basting and grilling its inhabitants. And, since that first clam, I've continued to gravitate toward seafood at its freshest and most simple, like my Sashimi-Style Raw Fish with Sushi Rice (page 159) and Mackerel in Lemon Broth (page 156). I turn to fish as a healthy weeknight meal, like Salmon with Soy & Ginger (page 169). But, what I love most is to make shellfish for my friends—not only because I adore shellfish, but also because it kills any awkward pretension that might happen during a dinner party. A dish that's messy and forces you to use your hands, like Peel & Eat Shrimp with Garlic & Parsley (page 181) or my California Crab Boil (page 178), is the best activity at any gathering (limbo aside).

This chapter is dedicated to the ocean—for giving me so many gifts over the years, for the thousands of fish I've served guests at my restaurants and at home, for the hundreds of bivalves I've ingested, greedily slurping their water and tossing their shell. And, above all—even above the food— for giving me a refuge when I've needed it most.

Mackerel in Lemon Broth

Serves 4 as a starter

1 leek, white and tender green
  parts only

¼ cup plus 1 tablespoon white
  wine vinegar

¼ cup white wine

2 sprigs flat-leaf parsley

4 black peppercorns

Juice of 1 lemon

1 medium carrot, peeled and
  halved horizontally

1 radish, very thinly sliced

Salt

1 small zucchini, very thinly sliced

8- to 10-ounce sushi-grade
  mackerel fillet

Extra-virgin olive oil

8 to 10 sprigs dill

8 to 10 sprigs chervil or fennel
  fronds (optional)

This is a light, refreshing appetizer that highlights the natural flavors of a piece of fish worthy of being served raw: be sure to only buy the best-quality mackerel you can get your hands on. Use a mandoline to slice the vegetables if you have one. If you don't, try to slice the vegetables as thinly as possible so their texture and flavor don't compete with the fish itself. From there get creative making pretty shapes with paper-thin vegetables.

In a small pot on high heat, combine the leek, vinegar, wine, parsley, peppercorns, lemon juice, a carrot half, and 2½ cups water. Bring to a simmer, then turn the heat to low and let the broth sit, uncovered, for 30 minutes. Strain the lemon broth into a bowl and let it cool to room temperature.

Meanwhile, very thinly slice the remaining half carrot. Soak the radish in cold water for 10 minutes to crisp.

Bring a large pot of water to a boil on high heat and set a bowl of ice water next to the pot. Once boiling, add salt to taste. Dunk the sliced carrot and zucchini into the boiling water for 30 seconds to blanch, then transfer immediately to the ice water to stop the cooking process. Set the vegetables aside on a paper towel to drain.

Remove the mackerel's skin using a sharp knife. Lightly sprinkle each side with salt and let rest at room temperature for 15 minutes.

Rinse the fish with cold water and pat dry. Cut the fillet in half horizontally so it's very thin, then cut the sliced fish vertically to make thin strips.

To serve, pour the cooled broth into a small serving bowl. Roll up the strips of fish like a fruit roll up, and set them on their side in the broth so you see a swirl shape from the top. Arrange the vegetables over and around the fish and in the broth. Finish with a drizzle of olive oil and garnish with the dill and chervil.

Pairs well with "The Song Is You" by Charlie Parker Quartet

Sashimi-Style Raw Fish with Sushi Rice

Serves 2 as a main, 4 as a starter

½ cup white soy sauce

½ cup extra-virgin olive oil

8 ounces sushi-grade fluke, amberjack, or sea bass, skin removed and cut into ½-inch strips

2 small radishes

2 large sheets nori

1 cup sushi rice

2 tablespoons finely chopped chives

White or black sesame seeds for sprinkling

Juice of 1 lime

This is one of my favorite ways to eat fish: lightly dressed and raw. I make the sushi rice according to my rice cooker's instructions and suggest that you do the same, but I have included my personalized rice-rinsing ritual here. You can take it or leave it, but I recommend you rinse your rice to remove excess starch and have some fun while doing so.

Whisk together the white soy sauce and olive oil in a large bowl. Add the fish, cover the bowl loosely with plastic wrap, and set in your refrigerator to chill.

Trim off the ends of the radishes. Use a sharp knife or mandoline to very thinly slice them. Stack the slices on top of each other and thinly slice the stacks lengthwise so each piece resembles a matchstick. Soak the radishes in ice water for 30 minutes to crisp, then drain and pat dry.

Meanwhile, turn the burner of your stove on high. Slowly wave each sheet of nori over the burner until it becomes fragrant and crispy but doesn't brown. Slice the toasted nori into thin strips, about 2 inches long by ¼ inch wide. Set aside.

To rinse the rice, cover it with cold water and rub the grains between your two palms, as if you're starting a fire with two sticks. Dump out the water (there's no need to use a strainer—gravity will force the rice to the bottom of the bowl and save you from washing an extra dish). Cover the rice with cold water again. Make your hand into a claw, lower it into the water, and whisk in a circular motion. Dump out the water. Cover the rice with cold water a third time and churn the rice by cupping your hands underneath it and turning your hands over. Dump out the water, which by now should have turned from a milky white to clear. Pour the rice into a rice cooker and cook according to the manufacturer's instructions. Let the rice cool to just slightly warm or room temperature.

To serve, spread the rice on your serving dish with the fish layered on top. Add the radishes, nori, chives, and a generous sprinkling of sesame seeds. Finish with a squeeze of lime.

Pairs well with "Slippin' and Slidin'" by Buddy Holly

Cod with Clams in a Green Sauce

Serves 4

1½ pounds Manila or littleneck clams, in the shell

1½ pounds Atlantic cod or black cod, preferably skin-on, cut into 4 pieces

All-purpose flour

Salt and freshly ground black pepper

¼ cup extra-virgin olive oil

2 cloves garlic, thinly sliced

2 tablespoons white wine

3 tablespoons chopped fresh flat-leaf parsley leaves

An old Basque recipe I picked up while cooking in Spain nearly thirty years ago, this cod with clams dish is all about slow and low: slowly cooking the fish at a low temperature to create a sauce without overcooking the cod. The clams release their juices and both hydrate and flavor the fish. What's great is that you only have to use one pot, and the dish requires very few ingredients; the green sauce is made only with parsley.

Rinse the clams thoroughly in cold water, then soak them in cold water for 30 minutes. Rinse thoroughly once more to remove any remaining sand, then drain and set aside, discarding any clams that have opened.

Coat the fish in flour. Sprinkle both sides of each piece with a pinch each of salt and pepper.

Pour the olive oil into a large pan and add the garlic and fish, skin-side down. Set the pan on low heat and cook gently, flipping the fish when the bottom just begins to color, about 2 minutes. Stir 2 teaspoons flour into the oil to form a roux. Turn the heat to medium. When the oil starts to bubble, stir in the wine, clams, parsley, and a pinch of salt. Cover the pan and turn the heat to low. Cook, shaking the pan occasionally to prevent the fish from sticking, until the fish is cooked through and the clams have opened, about 10 minutes.

Divide the fish among serving bowls, spooning plenty of cooking liquid over the top. Serve immediately.

Pairs well with *"Can't Seem to Make You Mine" by The Seeds*

Oven-Roasted Potatoes with Cod

Serves 4

1 ounce jamón Ibérico, prosciutto, or bacon, thinly sliced

¼ cup extra-virgin olive oil

1 white onion, thinly sliced

2 cloves garlic, crushed

2 russet potatoes, peeled and cut into ¼-inch slices

Salt

1½ pounds Atlantic cod, black cod, or sea bass, cut into 2-inch slices

Baked fish might inspire a boring weeknight feeling, but this slowly baked, tender cod served on top of potatoes flavored with ham fat is anything but—it's easy enough for a weeknight but tasty enough to share. If you're having friends over or just want to go the extra mile, serve this with Mother-Sauce Mayo (page 17) on the side. It's hard to believe that pork-flavored potatoes could get even better, but wait until you try pork-flavored potatoes with handmade mayonnaise.

Preheat your oven to 400°F.

In a large pan on low heat, cook the ham until it's crispy, about 6 minutes. Use a slotted spoon to transfer the ham to a paper towel to drain, leaving the fat in the pan. (If you don't have a slotted spoon, tilt the pan to one side, let the fat pool at the bottom, and scoop out the meat.)

With the fat still in the pan, turn the heat to medium-low. Stir in the olive oil, onion, and garlic. Cook until the onion is soft but hasn't taken on any color, about 10 minutes.

Stir in the potatoes, ham, and a pinch of salt. Cook, stirring frequently, until the potatoes sizzle and begin to brown, about 10 minutes.

Transfer the potato mixture to a small casserole or baking dish. Bake until the potatoes and onion have browned, stirring a couple of times to prevent any sticking on the bottom of the dish, about 20 minutes.

Remove the potatoes from your oven and lower the temperature to 275°F. Leave your oven door open for a few minutes to allow it to cool.

Set the fish on top of the potatoes and sprinkle with a pinch of salt. Return the potatoes and fish to your oven and bake until the fish is cooked through, about 20 minutes. Serve immediately.

Pairs well with *"Moonlight Mile" by The Rolling Stones*

Salmon en Papillote

Serves 4

2 teaspoons salt-packed capers

8 button mushrooms

1 fennel bulb, trimmed and thinly sliced

1 pint cherry tomatoes, halved

12 green olives, pitted and thinly sliced

1½ pounds salmon, skin removed and cut into four portions

2 tablespoons extra-virgin olive oil

4 tablespoons dry white wine

A handful of basil leaves

1 lemon, thinly sliced

Salt and freshly ground black pepper

Chopped fresh flat-leaf parsley for garnish

With this traditional method of cooking fish wrapped in parchment paper, the paper fills with steam and puffs up like a balloon. The salmon is cooked relatively quickly while remaining tender, but the best part of preparing something en papillote is when you tear open the paper, release the steam, and take in the aroma. I love the Mediterranean flavors of these vegetables, but feel free to substitute whatever vegetables, herbs, and citrus you have on hand.

Preheat your oven to 400°F.

In a fine-mesh strainer, rinse the capers in cold water, then soak them covered with cold water in a small bowl for 10 minutes to remove their salt. Drain and set aside.

Mushrooms absorb water like a sponge. Instead of rinsing, clean them by brushing off any dirt with a damp paper towel. Remove and discard their stems and thinly slice the caps.

Divide the vegetables into four portions, one for each piece of fish. Cut four pieces of parchment paper a bit more than double the size of one fish portion and fold each one in half. Unfold one piece of parchment paper and layer two slices of fennel on one-half of the paper as the base. Layer the mushrooms on top of the fennel. Set a piece of fish on top of the mushrooms, then sprinkle on the capers, cherry tomatoes, and olives. Douse with ½ tablespoon of the olive oil and 1 tablespoon of the white wine. Top with the basil leaves, lemon slices, and a healthy pinch each of salt and pepper.

Refold the parchment paper to cover the fish. Starting on one side, fold the parchment paper up in shallow triangles, working your way around the unfinished edge until you've sealed the paper packet on all sides. Fold the final triangle down to force the "pillow" you've created to lie flat. Repeat with the remaining three portions of fish. Place the paper pillows on a large baking sheet and bake for 14 minutes.

Remove the baking sheet from your oven. Use scissors to carefully open each paper packet and discard the lemon slices. Push the fish and its accoutrements onto plates, sliding the paper out from beneath each one. Garnish with parsley and serve immediately.

Pairs well with "Hey Joe" by Johnny Hallyday

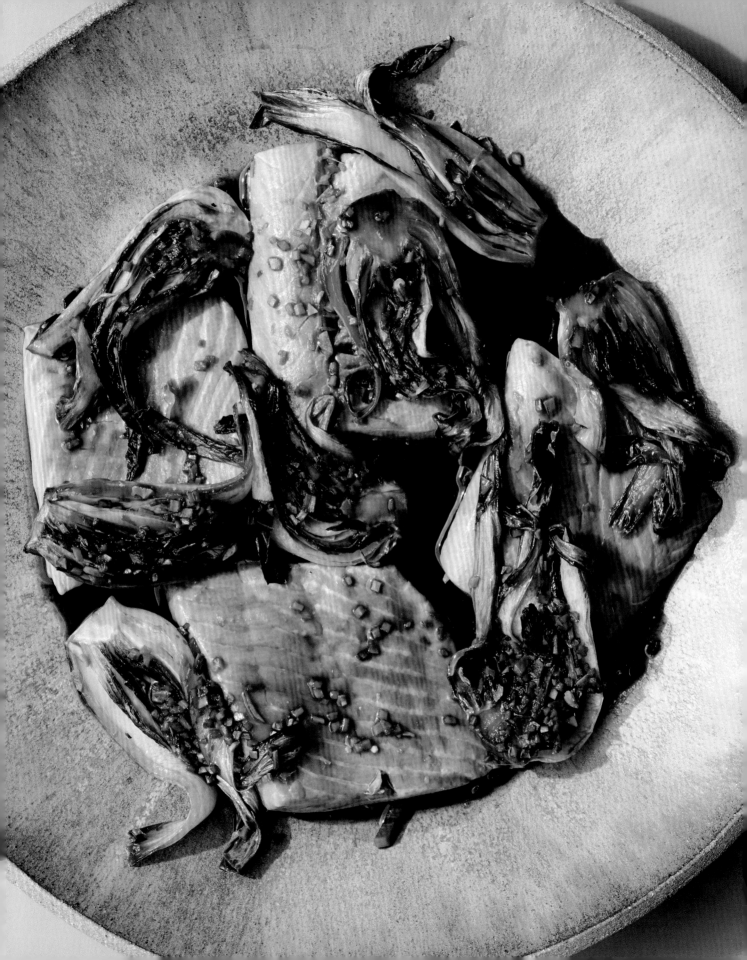

Salmon with Soy & Ginger

Serves 4

6 heads baby bok choy

1 tablespoon sunflower oil

2-inch piece fresh ginger,
   peeled and finely diced

3 cloves garlic, finely chopped

½ cup "lite" or low-sodium soy sauce

1½ pounds salmon fillet, cut into four
   equal portions

This simple gingery and garlicky salmon is unassuming, but
sneakily delicious. It's one of those dishes you learn to make
once—and it sticks with you. You'll make it over and over again,
barely needing to check this page for instruction. Be sure to use
a low-sodium soy sauce or the salmon and bok choy both will
be too salty. Though very weeknight-for-one and leftovers-later
friendly, if you make this for your friends, they'll see it come
together in twenty minutes and then ask for the recipe.

Remove any tough outer leaves from the bok choy. Trim off the bottom
stem and tops, being careful not to trim the stem too high or it will fall
apart. Cut each head in half lengthwise.

Heat the sunflower oil in a large pan on medium heat. When the oil is hot,
place the bok choy, cut-side down, in the pan. Cook, nudging the bok choy
every so often to prevent sticking, until it has browned and caramelized
at the bottom, about 5 minutes.

Turn the heat to low and add the ginger, garlic, and soy sauce. Gently
stir to combine, keeping the bok choy cut-side down. Cover the pan and
simmer until the bok choy has softened, about 5 minutes.

Remove the bok choy and set it aside. With the heat still on low, place the
salmon, skin-side down, in the pan and cover. Cook for 5 minutes, then
uncover the pan and tilt it so the soy sauce pools at the bottom. Use a
spoon to ladle the soy sauce, garlic, and ginger over the top of the salmon
to baste it. Return the bok choy to the pan, cover, and continue to cook
until the salmon is cooked through, 5 minutes more.

Transfer the salmon to a cutting board. Carefully remove the skin if desired.
Serve the salmon with a spoonful of the soy ginger sauce and a head or
two of bok choy.

Pairs well with "Elevator Operator" by Gene Clark with The Gosdin Brothers

Salmon with Pea & Mint Pesto

Serves 4

1½ pounds salmon fillet

Extra-virgin olive oil

Kosher salt

1½ cups frozen peas

1 cup mint leaves

½ cup chopped garlic

⅓ cup walnuts

½ cup finely grated Pecorino Romano

Flaky sea salt and freshly ground black pepper

It helps to know: **This recipe requires a food processor or blender.**

I think of this as a light spring or summer weeknight meal, but since peas are the one vegetable I don't mind using frozen, you can really make this pesto all year round. Spread any leftovers on crostini, stir into pasta, or use with anything as you would a traditional pesto.

Preheat your oven to 225°F and line a baking dish with aluminum foil.

Brush the salmon with a thin layer of olive oil and set it in the prepared dish, skin-side down. Sprinkle the top with a pinch of kosher salt, and bake for 5 minutes. Remove the dish from your oven, turn the fish over, and peel off and discard its skin. Return the dish to your oven and bake until the salmon is medium-rare, about 10 minutes more.

Meanwhile, in a food processor or blender, pulse together the peas, mint, garlic, walnuts, and a pinch of salt until a rough paste forms. Turn the speed to low and slowly add olive oil until you've reached your desired consistency (6 to 8 tablespoons). Add the Pecorino and pulse until combined.

To serve, spread the pea pesto on a serving plate and top with the baked salmon. Sprinkle with flaky sea salt and pepper to taste.

Pairs well with *"La nuit n'en finit plus" by Petula Clark*

Spicy Snapper Ceviche

Serves 4 as a starter

12 ounces snapper fillet, skinned
and bones removed

1 large ruby red grapefruit

¼ cup freshly squeezed lime juice
(about 4 limes)

Salt

1 (13.5-ounce) can coconut milk
(not "lite")

1 red onion, halved and thinly sliced

2 teaspoons chopped cilantro leaves

1 jalapeño, seeded and finely chopped

1 serrano chile, seeded and finely
chopped (optional)

Fresh flat-leaf parsley for garnish
(optional)

This ceviche makes a refreshing lunch or a starter to a heavier meal. One finished, the dressing and juice left in the bowl are so delicious that you'll find yourself wanting to slurp it up (my favorite friends are the ones who do). Feel free to prepare this up to 4 hours in advance and store it covered in your refrigerator until you are ready to serve.

Slice the snapper into ¼-inch-wide strips and set them aside in a large bowl.

Using a sharp knife, peel the grapefruit and cut out its segments over a bowl to reserve the juice. Set aside the segments, and stir the lime juice and a pinch of salt into the grapefruit juice. Pour the mixture over the fish, cover, and refrigerate for 1 hour. The juice will cure the fish and turn it a milky-white color.

Shake the can of coconut milk to combine its cream and water.

Take the fish out of the fridge, drain off any excess juice, and gently stir in the onion, cilantro, jalapeño, serrano, and grapefruit segments. Stir in enough of the coconut milk to just coat the ingredients (you may not use the whole can as you don't want it to be soupy). Set the mixture aside for 15 minutes to allow the onion to break down and the flavors to come together.

Garnish with parsley and serve.

Pairs well with "Batida diferente" by Herbie Mann

Oyster Stew

Serves 4 as a starter

4 cups whole milk

½ cup butter

1 tablespoon freshly ground
   black pepper

Salt

24 shucked oysters in their water

1 bunch chives, cut into ½-inch pieces

Garlicky Herbed Croutons (page 26)

This stew is absurdly simple: just oysters in milk and butter. It is New England fisherman food, but there's something elegant about it—maybe it's that slick of butter that rests on top. Plus, it comes together in under 10 minutes.

In a large pot on medium heat, stir together the milk and butter. When the butter has melted and combined with the milk, season with the pepper and a healthy pinch of salt.

Bring the milk to a simmer, stir in the oysters, their water, and the chives. Cook until the oysters start to curl around the edges, about 1 minute.

To serve, divide the stew among four bowls and top with croutons.

Pairs well with *"Hoe Down" by Oliver Nelson*

How I Became a Californian

My path to California was a roundabout one, beginning with the realization that, after six years, I needed to get the hell out of New York City. It was the 1980s and I was making just enough money to not only get by, but also embrace the lifestyle. I came home very late one August night and dragged my mattress to the fire escape, desperate for just enough air to be able to sleep. The next morning, I woke up at 7 a.m. to the sound of some guy playing his boom box at full volume directly outside my window. It was 102°F and humid. I thought to myself, "Fuck, that's it." That exact moment would likely have been charming in year one, but the novelty had worn off.

A few years earlier, Barry Wine, the chef/owner of the Quilted Giraffe and an important mentor of mine, had returned from a trip to Japan, bringing with him a fascination for the culture that trickled its way into the food and, consequently, into the minds of the entire kitchen staff. Barry was using Japanese techniques and flavors in a New American restaurant before anyone in New York was doing the same—before the term "Asian Fusion" had become so trendy that it turned passé. It was new and revolutionary, and I was hooked.

I left New York for Fukuoka, Japan, the largest city on the northern shore of Kyushu, where a regular customer of mine had set me up with a job. I was hired to cook Western food in a restaurant that primarily served Japanese businesspeople, but I became good friends with the general manager, who gave me an extensive education in Japanese culture. He took me out every single night (I'm not being hyperbolic—we were young). We'd go to bars and clubs and sumo tournaments and tiny restaurants hidden in alleyways or way out in the countryside. He took me to yakitori spots, restaurants devoted to serving only chicken, some of which the chefs raised themselves. At one such restaurant, I tried chicken sashimi, a regional dish of, yep, raw chicken. It was a divine bite of the torpedo-shaped meat under the breast known as the tenderloin, dipped into boiling dashi for just enough time to sear and sterilize the surface while retaining a completely raw center. It was a remarkably wild bite of chicken that you would be hard-pressed to find at any American restaurant to this day—it's a bite I'll never forget.

I wanted Japan to be my home; I was studying the language and making a life for myself when my work visa expired and I was forced to leave. I moved in with my parents in the East Bay and started commuting to work in San Francisco on the BART train. I became the executive chef at a fine-dining restaurant in the city at twenty-seven, but something still wasn't right. I had chased money, and I wasn't ready. I knew I still had too much to learn if I was going to accomplish my true ambitions.

A few scary but ultimately lucky moments forced me to leave California. First, I nearly drowned while surfing at Ocean Beach. That break is no joke. On a big day, it has a certain way of forcing you to reevaluate your life choices. Shortly after, the earthquake of 1989 hit and the city halted. Restaurants, including mine, were empty. I sold what I had, pulled my savings, and started from scratch.

I set out to travel around the world overland. I started in Hong Kong and worked my way through Southeast Asia, China, and the former Soviet Union, passing through seventeen countries on my way to Western Europe. I spent the next two years in what I consider "finishing school," staging in vineyards and kitchens in France, Germany, and Spain. I had gone from an executive chef—ahead for my years by most standards—to a twenty-seven-year-old stage, and it was the best decision I ever made.

Despite a few "what am I doing?" moments, during my years of traveling solo, I never really felt lonely. I became friends with the kitchen crew in each country, some of whom I remain in contact with to this day. I learned as much as I could about the language native to where I was staying. I ate at people's homes, or on the street sitting on tiny plastic stools, or in beautiful dining rooms, or sitting on the curb in the alleyway behind a restaurant. No matter where I went, food was at the heart of the culture. It was powerful.

As these romantic stories often go, I woke up one day and accepted that I was out of money. I returned to California with a collection of dishes and experiences I will cherish for the rest of my life, ready for the next adventure: to cook in my own restaurant.

California Crab Boil

Serves 6 to 8

2 white onions

1 (750-ml) bottle dry white wine

1 (750-ml) bottle verjus (optional; just leave it out if you can't find it)

⅓ cup apple cider vinegar

1 tablespoon coriander seeds

2 tablespoons fennel seeds

3 cloves garlic

2 lemons, sliced

¾ cup salt

1 teaspoon black peppercorns

6 quarts (24 cups) water

4 to 8 whole Dungeness crabs (about ½ crab per person, and then some, for the overachievers), rinsed well with cold water

1¼ pounds baby potatoes

It helps to know: This recipe requires an extra-large pot (I'm not messing around here, you need a big one).

You can keep things simple and blanch fresh crab in salted water, or you can go in a different direction and make something really flavorful. The boil can be prepared a day in advance so you just have to cook the shellfish when you're ready. Eat the crab and potatoes on their own or with Mother-Sauce Mayo (page 17) on the side. What makes this a California crab boil, you ask? It's meant to be eaten outdoors in the winter and washed down with an ice-cold California Chardonnay (I like Mount Eden Vineyards, close by in the Santa Cruz Mountains).

First, char the onions. This step is optional, but it adds a nice smoky flavor to the boil. Cut off the ends of the onions (you can leave the skin on), then slice each in half. Line a pan (cast iron, if you have it) with aluminum foil and place it on high heat. Lay the onions on the pan, cut-side down, and let them sit without nudging until the cut side turns black, about 12 minutes. Remove the onions' outer skin.

In an extra-large pot on high heat, combine the onions, wine, verjus, vinegar, coriander, fennel, garlic, lemons, salt, peppercorns, and the water and bring to a boil. Turn the heat to low and simmer, uncovered, for 20 minutes.

Remove the pot from the heat and let it cool to room temperature. Strain the stock into another large pot, discarding the solids. The resulting liquid is called a "crab court-bouillon," or a flavored stock for poaching crab. Use immediately, or store the bouillon, covered, in your refrigerator for up to 24 hours.

Just before serving, bring the strained stock to a boil on high heat. Once boiling, add the crabs and potatoes. Boil, uncovered, for 8 minutes. Remove the pot from the heat and let it cool to room temperature with the potatoes and crab still in the pot. Drain.

Line your table (ideally outdoors) with newspaper. Dump the crab and potatoes on the newspaper. Eat with your hands, leaving the shells on the newspapers to be neatly folded up and tossed when no crabmeat or potatoes remain.

Pairs well with "California Soul" by Marlena Shaw

Peel & Eat Shrimp with Garlic & Parsley

Serves 6

Extra-virgin olive oil

1 cup fresh flat-leaf parsley leaves, finely chopped

2 cloves garlic, finely chopped

½ teaspoon red pepper flakes

Salt and freshly ground black pepper

1 pound extra jumbo (16/20) shrimp in shells, rinsed well with cold water

This dish is messy, fun to eat, and easy to make. I like to rip off the tail and eat the shrimp whole in its shell, dipped in Mother-Sauce Mayo (page 17).

In a large bowl, stir together ½ cup olive oil, the parsley, garlic, red pepper flakes, and 1 teaspoon each salt and pepper. Reserve ¼ cup of the marinade, and stir the shrimp into the remaining marinade. Cover and set aside at room temperature for 30 minutes to 1 hour.

In a large pan on high heat, add olive oil to cover the bottom in a thin film. When the oil begins to shimmer, add the shrimp, its marinade, and a pinch of salt. Cook on high, stirring often, until the shrimp turn a whitish color and no longer look raw, 5 to 6 minutes.

Transfer the cooked shrimp to a large bowl, add the reserved marinade, and toss to coat. Serve along with plenty of napkins as soon as the shrimp are cool enough to peel.

Pairs well with "Pots on, Gas on High" by John Lee Hooker

Trout with Fennel & Grapefruit

Serves 4

2 ruby red grapefruits

Extra-virgin olive oil

2 fennel bulbs, cut vertically
    into ½-inch slices

1 sprig thyme

Salt

2 tablespoons dry white wine

2 pounds skin-on trout fillets

Fish with fennel and citrus is a classic combination. This dish (which uses only one pan!) features grapefruit, a slight variation from the lemon that's more commonly used. My father used to eat grapefruit for breakfast every morning, and I still remember the first time he gave me a bite to taste. The shockingly bright citrus was almost as transformative as my first steamed clam. Be it nostalgia or otherwise, it's been one of my favorite fruits ever since. I adore the trout I buy from my local seafood market, but I know it can be hard to find. Cod, salmon, sea bass, or even scallops work well as a substitute.

Peel the grapefruits using a sharp knife, then cut out the segments over a bowl to reserve the juice. Set aside.

In a large pan on low heat, add enough olive oil to cover the bottom in a thin film. Add the fennel, thyme, and a pinch of salt. Cook, stirring occasionally, until the fennel softens and lightly caramelizes, about 10 minutes.

Turn the heat to high and add the wine to deglaze the pan. Add the grapefruit juice and stir to combine. Turn the heat to low.

Slice diagonal lines about 1 inch apart into the trout's skin, deep enough to just pierce the skin but not the flesh. This prevents the skin from shrinking as it cooks. Season the fish with a pinch of salt on each side.

Push the fennel to the edges of the pan, add the fish skin-side down, and cover. Cook for 3 minutes, then flip the trout, cover, and cook for 3 minutes more. Turn off the heat to steam the fish through, about 3 minutes more.

Transfer to a large platter and serve immediately.

Pairs well with *"The Tide Is High" by The Paragons*

MEAT + VEGETABLES

Meat and vegetables may seem like an unlikely pairing in a cookbook chapter, but the two have played complementary and competing roles my entire life. I was raised eating meat at nearly every meal. Vegetables, on the other hand, were served as an afterthought, never the focus. They've switched places as I've gotten older, and my feelings on meat have evolved. I've found myself gravitating toward lighter dishes and a more vegetable- and fish-heavy diet. Meat has gone from a major staple to playing a more supportive role.

Today, I eat meat only on occasion. I believe the way in which the animal is raised affects not only its well-being, but also the sustainability and quality of the product. Animals that are treated humanely and fed a proper diet, whose health and happiness are maintained, taste better, but it's an expensive proposition. As such, I treat high-quality meat as an investment. It's a luxury product. And if you know me, you know that I'm all for luxury in moderation.

My relationship with vegetables has also deepened with time. In fact, they've played a crucial role in dictating my life choices. The first time I visited a farmers' market in California, I was shocked by what I found on the stands. It reminded me of Europe: the produce was exceptional, and the farmers took great pride in what they were selling. It was one of the main reasons I chose to open my first restaurant in California, and why I made the state my home. I love cooking vegetables; I love their diversity, seasonality, and range of colors and textures. The possibilities are limitless, leaving me continuously inspired.

Though this chapter is an extension of my own relationship with meat and vegetables, the two are given equal significance. The meat recipes are celebratory: lively and exciting, like my Duck Breast with Braised Red Cabbage & Dried Figs (page 189), or full of emotional significance and comfort, like my Roast Chicken (page 202). While I treasure these recipes, the vegetables are just as enticing, like my Ratatouille, Hot or Cold, Poached Egg or Not (page 209). Of course, many dishes prove that meat and vegetables taste best together, like my Belgian Endive Gratin (page 207) complete with plenty of ham and cheese.

When it comes down to it, this chapter is a celebration of quality—of vegetables in excess and of luxury in moderation. And, like many things in my life, it's a hope of finding the balance between the two.

6

Pork Tenderloins with Coriander & Fennel

Serves 6 to 8

2 tablespoons fennel seeds

1 tablespoon coriander seeds

½ teaspoon black peppercorns

2 pork tenderloins
   (about 1 pound each)

Extra-virgin olive oil

1 small head green cabbage

Salt

2 tablespoons butter

2 sprigs thyme

4 cloves garlic, crushed

Cabbage is delicious, nutritious, cheap, and highly underrated. You can shred it and add some vinegar and mayonnaise for a refreshing coleslaw, or caramelize it in butter for a savory side to a well-cooked roast meat, as I've done here. And speaking of well-cooked meat, here's a small caveat: be careful not to overcook the pork. A dry, overcooked tenderloin is a sad prospect. A juicy tenderloin, cooked to a medium temperature, as instructed in this recipe, is just right.

In a small pan on low heat, lightly toast the fennel and coriander, tossing constantly, until they take on some color and become fragrant, about 3 minutes. Transfer to a plate to cool.

Crush the toasted spices and the peppercorns using a mortar and pestle, then spread them on a cutting board. If you don't have a mortar and pestle, crush them by pressing down and forward firmly with the bottom of a pot.

Rub the tenderloins with olive oil, then roll them in the spices to coat on all sides. Cover with plastic wrap and marinate in your refrigerator for at least 1 hour, or better yet, overnight.

Preheat your oven to 350°F. Remove the tenderloins from your refrigerator and let them come to room temperature before roasting.

Remove the outer leaves of the cabbage and slice it in half. Leaving the core intact, slice each half lengthwise into 1-inch-wide planks. Set aside.

Heat 1 tablespoon olive oil in a large ovenproof pan on medium heat. Sprinkle the tenderloins with a couple generous pinches of salt. Sear, turning until they've browned on all sides, about 5 minutes total.

Transfer to your oven and roast until the pork is cooked to medium (about 145°F), 9 to 11 minutes. Set aside on a plate, covered with aluminum foil, to rest for 20 minutes.

Meanwhile, melt the butter in a medium pan on medium heat. Once melted, turn the heat to low and add the cabbage in one layer. Add the thyme, garlic, and a pinch of salt. Cover and let the cabbage caramelize without nudging until the pieces are soft and nicely browned, about 20 minutes. Carefully flip the cabbage onto a serving plate to expose the browned side.

To serve, cut the pork horizontally into ¾-inch-wide slices and arrange next to the cabbage, pouring any juices that have pooled over the top.

Pairs well with "Line between Love and Hate" by the Wallace Brothers

Duck Breast with Braised Red Cabbage & Dried Figs

Serves 6

BRAISED RED CABBAGE

⅔ cup dry red wine

½ cup port wine

3 tablespoons red wine vinegar

2-inch piece fresh ginger, sliced into 3 pieces (you can leave the peel on)

8 dried figs, halved

Sugar

Salt

1 medium head red cabbage, quartered, core discarded, and thinly sliced

⅓ cup extra-virgin olive oil

2 medium white onions, thinly sliced

DUCK

4 boned duck breasts (6 to 8 ounces each)

Neutral oil, such as sunflower or grapeseed

Salt and freshly ground black pepper

Roast Shallots in Space (page 31) for serving (optional)

It helps to know: This cabbage marinates overnight.

I encourage you to make this recipe your own. Don't be limited by the ingredients listed here: other dried fruits would work well in place of the figs: apricots, pears, or even something wild like pineapple. If you don't like duck breast, this cabbage is also tasty alongside any meat—especially pork. If you do like duck breast but you're scared to cook it, my advice is simple: don't be. This method is easy and takes less than 20 minutes.

To make the cabbage, in a large bowl, stir together the red wine, port wine, vinegar, ginger, figs, and a pinch each of sugar and salt. Add the cabbage and toss until well coated. Cover and let marinate in your refrigerator overnight.

When ready to serve, preheat your oven to 325°F. Remove the duck from your refrigerator and let it come to room temperature before cooking.

Warm the olive oil in a large ovenproof pan on medium heat. Add the onions and cook until they've softened and just begun to turn golden, about 12 minutes. Stir in the cabbage mixture along with its marinade. Cover and bake for 45 minutes. Remove the cover, stir, and bake for another 45 minutes, uncovered. The cabbage will be quite tender and soft, with almost the consistency of a spread.

Meanwhile, about 30 minutes before serving, trim off any fat that surrounds the perimeter of the duck breasts. Starting at one corner, with the skin side facing up, use a sharp knife to cut diagonal lines in the duck's skin about ¼ inch apart. Repeat, starting at the opposite corner to make a diamond pattern. This allows the fat that's just beneath the skin to escape as you cook.

In a medium pan on low heat, add enough neutral oil to cover the bottom in a thin film. Once the oil begins to shimmer (but before it gets very hot), set the duck breasts in the pan skin-side down. You should hear the soft sound of the skin crisping—if it's loud, your pan is likely too hot. Let the meat sit without nudging until the skin is dark brown and crispy, about 8 minutes.

Sprinkle the flesh side liberally with salt and pepper. Turn the breasts over and allow to gently sizzle for 1 minute. Transfer to your cutting board to rest, uncovered, for 5 minutes.

Cut the duck into ½-inch-wide slices. Transfer the cabbage to a serving bowl and remove the ginger. Add some roast shallots, top with the sliced duck, and serve.

Pairs well with "Catfish Blues" by John Littlejohn

Lamb Tartare

Serves 4 as a starter

12 ounces leg of lamb

3 anchovy fillets (oil-packed),
 or 3 raw oysters, coarsely
 chopped (optional)

1 tablespoon capers

1 teaspoon Dijon mustard

1 egg yolk

1 tablespoon extra-virgin olive oil

1 tablespoon chopped mint leaves

Zest of 1 lemon

1 shallot, finely chopped

Freshly ground black pepper

Flaky sea salt

Though some may find leg of lamb to be too chewy, I like it for a tartare because it has so much flavor. Because it's sliced so thinly, even the highly sensitive can appreciate the taste without being turned off by the texture. I love lamb with anchovies, but my absolute favorite way to serve it is with oysters—or both, if you're willing to be adventurous. Feel free to leave them out (or use a rack of lamb and no egg yolk if you really want to play it safe). This dish is super easy to make, just be sure to thoroughly chill the meat or it will be difficult to slice. Serve the tartare with grilled bread or raw endive spears broken apart into cups, or, my personal favorite, crisp salty potato chips.

Trim off and discard any silvery white fat from the lamb. Slice it thinly into ¼-inch strips, then stack the strips on top of each other and cut vertically into ¼-inch strips again. Turn the slices 90 degrees and cut vertically into ¼-inch cubes. Place the cubes in a bowl, cover, and chill in your refrigerator until just before you're ready to serve.

In a fine-mesh strainer, rinse the anchovies and capers in cold water, then soak them covered with cold water in a small bowl for 10 minutes to remove their salt. Drain and coarsely chop.

In a large bowl, combine the mustard, egg yolk, olive oil, and anchovies and whisk until incorporated.

Just before serving, stir the capers, mint, lemon zest, and shallot into the lamb. Add a pinch of pepper and mix gently to combine, fluffing the lamb with a fork to break apart the pieces. Fold in the egg yolk mixture and season with flaky sea salt to taste.

Serve immediately.

Pairs well with *"Motor Bikin'" by Chris Spedding*

Lamb Meatballs in an Almond & Pepper Sauce

Serves 6 to 8

MEATBALLS

1 small white onion

1 pound ground lamb

2 cloves garlic, finely chopped

2 heaping tablespoons finely chopped fresh dill

⅓ cup chopped fresh flat-leaf parsley leaves

1 egg, beaten

Zest of 1 lemon

½ teaspoon cayenne

1 teaspoon salt

Freshly ground black pepper

⅓ cup extra-virgin olive oil for frying

SAUCE

3 dried ancho chiles

2 tablespoons dried bread crumbs

2 cloves garlic, crushed

1 cup blanched sliced almonds, toasted (see page 83)

Salt

3 tomatoes (Early Girl or Roma preferred), peeled (see page 146)

1 roasted red bell pepper, finely chopped (jarred is okay)

½ cup extra-virgin olive oil

1 tablespoon sherry vinegar

It helps to know: **This recipe requires a food processor or blender.**

With fresh dill, parsley, and lemon zest, these easy lamb meatballs have a tasty Mediterranean flavor that goes well with a romesco-style sauce. I like to keep the almond and pepper sauce in my refrigerator to use as a dip or to spread on just about anything—toast, grilled meats, you name it. I recommend you make plenty of extra. It will keep, covered, in your refrigerator for up to 1 week, but I doubt it will last that long.

To make the meatballs, grate the onion into a large bowl using the large side of a box grater. Add the lamb, garlic, dill, parsley, egg, lemon zest, cayenne, salt, and a couple large pinches of black pepper. Use your hands to mix everything together until just combined. Form the mixture into meatballs each about the size of a golf ball and refrigerate for 1 hour to firm. Don't skimp on this step; they'll fall apart if you try to fry them immediately.

Meanwhile, to make the sauce, remove the stems from the ancho chiles, break them in half, and discard their seeds. Soak them in a bowl of warm water for 30 minutes to soften. Drain, chop, and set aside.

In a small pan over low heat, toast the bread crumbs until they begin to brown, 5 to 7 minutes. Set aside.

In a food processor or blender, pulse together the garlic, almonds, and a couple pinches of salt until a rough paste forms. Squeeze out the tomato seeds over the sink to discard, then add the tomatoes to the paste along with the chiles, roasted red bell pepper, and bread crumbs. With the speed on low, slowly drizzle in the olive oil until all of it is incorporated. Transfer to a bowl, stir in the sherry vinegar, and season with salt to taste.

Preheat your oven to 350°F.

Coat the bottom of a large pan with olive oil and set over medium heat. When the oil is hot, add the meatballs in a single layer, carefully turning them until browned on all sides, about 1 minute per side. Work in batches, setting the browned meatballs aside on a paper towel.

Set the meatballs in a large baking dish and bake until cooked through, about 12 minutes.

Spread the almond and pepper sauce on your serving plate and top with the meatballs. Serve.

Pairs well with "Double Barrel" by Dave and Ansell Collins

Garlic & Ginger Grilled Chicken

Serves 6

12 ounces garlic cloves (you can just buy the peeled kind)

12 ounces fresh ginger, peeled and cut into 1-inch pieces

1¼ cups extra-virgin olive oil

½ cup toasted sesame oil (cold-pressed preferred)

6 bone-in, skin-on chicken thighs

Freshly ground black pepper

Salt

It helps to know: This recipe requires cheesecloth and a blender or food processor, and the chicken marinates for 6 hours.

Meant to be grilled outdoors on a warm night, these festive chicken thighs bring about that summer feeling almost as much as a fully ripe tomato. In this method, the oil-based marinade is poured into a bowl and covered with cheesecloth, and the thighs are placed on top. The oil infuses the meat, so you get all the flavor of the marinade without ruining the look of a simple summer grilled chicken. If you don't have a grill, this marinade also works well for cooking chicken in your oven or skillet.

In a food processor or blender, pulse the ginger and garlic until combined. Turn the speed to low and slowly drizzle in the olive oil until a paste forms.

Scrape the paste into a pan on medium heat and cook, stirring frequently, until the oil separates and the mixture turns from smooth to grainy, 10 to 15 minutes. Pour the mixture into a bowl and let it cool to room temperature.

Once cool, stir in the sesame oil and scrape into a dish large enough to hold all of the chicken thighs in one single layer. Drape a large piece of cheesecloth over the marinade.

Place the thighs skin-side up on top of the cheesecloth and season liberally with pepper. Marinate the chicken in your refrigerator for 3 hours, flip, and marinate for another 3 hours.

When you're ready to grill, remove the chicken from your refrigerator and let it come to room temperature before cooking. Build a pyramid shape with your coals, light them, and be patient. (Alternatively, turn a gas grill to low heat.) The key to a nicely grilled chicken is a low, even heat. When the coals are fully lit and about half of them have turned white, spread them into a single layer and wait for the coals to turn completely white with no red or orange glow.

Just before grilling, liberally season the chicken on both sides with salt. Place it skin-side down on the grates and grill until the fat renders and the skin crisps and turns brown, 10 to 15 minutes. Once the skin has crisped, flip and continue to grill until the chicken has cooked through, about 2 minutes more. Cooking times will depend greatly on the size of your chicken thighs, so take the timing as an estimate and make sure to keep an eye on things. Standing around the grill is part of the fun after all.

Transfer the grilled chicken to a serving platter and serve immediately.

Pairs well with "A Train, a Banjo, and a Chicken Wing" by Wynton Marsalis

The Fond

There are three main types of surfable waves: a point break, a reef break, and a beach break, but there's something particularly magical about a beach break. The sand shifts mysteriously beneath the ocean's surface, pulling and ebbing and moving to form sandbars on the seafloor. The pattern differs depending on nature: the tide, currents, and storms all affect the makeup of the seabed, which determines the way the waves break on the surface. It's always changing, but when the sandbar lines up, and the surf is working, it's one of nature's simplest gifts. Like most things I've chased throughout my life, a beach break is both magnificent and fleeting. It can last for weeks or for days, and failing to take advantage of it would be a shame.

I revere the fond—the dark bits that stick to the bottom of a pan as meat and vegetables brown, their juices dripping and sugars caramelizing—with a similar sense of awe: a small gift from nature that we, as pleasure-seeking mammals with far too many tools at our disposal, would be foolish to pass up.

French for "base," the fond is at the heart of French cuisine: it's the foundation of flavor. The dark golden bubbles of concentrated flavor are an opportunity: add some wine, vinegar, or even water over high heat, scrape them up from the bottom of the pan, and the result is transformative.

I encourage you to take full advantage of beach breaks, of fonds, and of all the small perfect gifts that nature gives us, for months, weeks, or sometimes just a few precious seconds.

Chicken Thighs with Dried Fruit

Serves 4

4 bone-in, skin-on chicken thighs

Salt

All-purpose flour

Extra-virgin olive oil

1 white onion, medium diced

1 clove garlic, chopped

1 cinnamon stick

1 bay leaf

½ cup sweet Muscat wine

½ cup Chicken Stock (page 32),
   Chickpea Stock (page 34), or water

¼ cup white wine vinegar

2 ounces dried mango

¼ cup golden raisins

12 dried apricots

¼ cup whole blanched almonds,
   lightly toasted (see page 83)

¼ cup blanched hazelnuts, halved and
   lightly toasted (see page 83)

2 teaspoons pine nuts, lightly toasted
   (see page 83)

12 seedless green grapes

It helps to know: **If you can't find blanched (unpeeled) hazelnuts, toast them whole and then rub them together in a clean kitchen towel to remove the skins.**

This chicken makes an easy weeknight dinner, especially when served with rice on the side. That said, it's tasty enough to be suitable for any dinner party. The sauce is delightful, and it rehydrates the dried fruit in a way that will have you searching the pan for any pieces of fruit left behind.

Season the chicken thighs on each side with a healthy pinch of salt, then coat each thigh with flour.

In a large pan on medium heat, add enough olive oil to cover the bottom in a thin film. When the oil is hot, place the thighs in the pan, skin-side down, and cook, nudging every so often to prevent sticking, until the skin turns golden brown, 10 to 12 minutes.

Flip the chicken, add the onion, and cook until the onion is softened, about 5 minutes. Add the garlic, cinnamon stick, and bay leaf and stir to combine. Cook until the garlic softens, 2 to 3 minutes.

Add the wine, turn the heat to high, and cook until the wine is almost completely evaporated. Add the stock and vinegar and bring the mixture to a simmer. Add the dried mango, raisins, apricots, and the toasted nuts, and turn the heat to low. Cover the pot with the lid slightly ajar to allow steam to escape. Simmer for 10 minutes.

Add the grapes and simmer until the chicken is cooked through, about 15 minutes.

To serve, transfer the chicken to serving plates, scooping up plenty of the juices and spooning the fruit and nuts over the top.

Pairs well with "Do the Do" by Howlin' Wolf

Chicken Thighs with Olives & Green Beans

Serves 6

1½ cups all-purpose flour

1 tablespoon espelette pepper
or hot paprika

1½ tablespoons smoked paprika

1 teaspoon freshly ground
black pepper

Salt

6 bone-in, skin-on chicken thighs

2 tablespoons extra-virgin olive oil

1 white onion, halved lengthwise,
then thinly sliced lengthwise

12 cloves garlic

Leaves from 2 sprigs thyme

2 bay leaves

¾ cup sherry vinegar

¾ cup dry white wine

¾ cup Chicken Stock (page 32),
Chickpea Stock (page 34), or water

12 green beans, ends trimmed

1 cup Taggiasca or Niçoise olives,
rinsed and left whole with their pits

In this French-style recipe, you render the fat from chicken thighs slowly, which leads to the ultimate goal when cooking chicken: a tender center and crispy skin. A high-quality olive with its pit goes a long way toward making this simple and homey dish of inexpensive chicken special nonetheless.

In a medium bowl, stir together the flour, espelette pepper, smoked paprika, black pepper, and 2 tablespoons salt. Coat each chicken thigh on all sides with the flour and spice mixture.

Heat the olive oil in a large pan on medium low heat. When the oil is hot, place the thighs in the pan skin-side down, working in batches as needed so the thighs don't touch one another. Cook, nudging occasionally to prevent sticking, until you hear the skin expel its water and turn a golden brown, about 12 minutes. You should hear a gentle, light sizzle. If it sounds louder than that, turn down the heat. Flip the thighs and continue to cook until the other side has browned, about 10 minutes more. Once you've browned each chicken thigh (the inside of the chicken hasn't been cooked through yet), transfer it to a plate and set aside.

Leaving the oil and chicken fat in the pan, turn the heat to medium and add the onion, garlic, thyme, and bay leaves and cook until the onion is soft and just starting to brown, about 10 minutes. You'll notice some dark brown and black bits on the bottom of the pan, which are the chicken's juices that have caramelized—this is the best part (see "The Fond" on page 196).

Return the browned chicken to the pan and turn the heat to high. Add the sherry vinegar to deglaze, scraping up the brown bits that have formed. Cook, stirring occasionally, until the liquid has evaporated.

Add the white wine and continue to cook, stirring occasionally, until the liquid has reduced by half, about 5 minutes. Add the stock, green beans, olives, and a pinch of salt and turn the heat to low. Cover the pan with the lid slightly ajar to allow steam to escape. Gently simmer until the chicken is cooked through, about 30 minutes. Taste and season with more salt, if necessary.

To serve, transfer the chicken to serving plates, scooping up plenty of the juices and spooning the green beans and olives over the top.

Pairs well with "Find Someone to Love" by Ohio Players

Roast Chicken

Serves 4 to 6

4½- to 5-pound chicken (if you use a 2- to 3-pound chicken, reduce the cooking times to about 15 minutes on each side, 10 minutes on its back)

½ cup butter, softened

Salt

STUFFING SUGGESTIONS

½ white onion, unpeeled

Leeks, trimmed

Lemons, sliced

Garlic cloves, peeled

Apples, cored and halved

Fresh flat-leaf parsley

Fresh sprigs thyme

VEGETABLE SUGGESTIONS

Baby potatoes

Turnips, peeled and halved

Leeks, trimmed and sliced

Celery root, peeled and chopped

Garlic cloves, unpeeled

Pearl onions, peeled

Carrots, peeled and chopped

Fresh sprigs thyme

Olive oil for coating

Salt and freshly ground black pepper

JUS (OPTIONAL)

½ cup dry white wine

Salt

It helps to know: **The chicken must sit for 24 hours before roasting.**

continued

A roast chicken is my favorite thing to make and to eat. Done correctly, I believe it's one of the grandest dishes of all time. In fact, there's very little I'd rather be doing than making a roast chicken for someone I love.

In other words, this recipe is the result of countless chickens that have passed through my home oven. If I've learned anything over many years of roasting chickens, it's to focus on the legs. Because the breast is exposed and has very little fat, the heat affects it quickly. The legs, being on the bone, cook slower, which leaves you fighting an undercooked leg or an overcooked breast.

For this reason, it's essential that you stuff the bird. An empty cavity will fill with hot air and cook the breast even faster. I have given some stuffing suggestions here, but you can stuff it with whatever you have on hand. You can even fill it with rolled-up balls of aluminum foil if necessary—anything to stop the heat from entering the chicken undisturbed.

Also, I roast the bird on each side to more aggressively cook the legs. Ideally you have a large Dutch oven so you can prop up the bird easily and use the resulting fond (page 196) to make a jus out of the caramelized drippings (though the jus is optional). If you don't have a Dutch oven, a roasting pan, flat baking sheet, or casserole dish will also work.

Remove any fat from the inside of the chicken and discard. Rinse the chicken inside and out with cold water and pat it thoroughly with paper towels to dry. Place the bird, uncovered, in your refrigerator for 24 hours to dry out its skin.

Remove the chicken from your refrigerator and let it come to room temperature before roasting. Preheat your oven to 450°F and place a roasting dish inside for 10 minutes to bring it to medium heat. This prevents sticking.

Stuff the cavity with the vegetables and herbs of your choice. Use your hands to coat the entire outside of the chicken with the butter, then sprinkle it liberally with salt.

Remove your roasting dish from your oven, and carefully set the chicken on its side, using the side of the dish for balance. Roast for 20 minutes, then use tongs to carefully flip the chicken onto its other side. Roast for another

20 minutes. Remove the pan from your oven and turn the temperature to 400°F. Leave your oven door open for 2 minutes to cool.

Use tongs to flip the bird onto its back so its breast is facing up. Toss the herbs and vegetables of your choice in a bowl with enough olive oil to coat and a pinch each of salt and pepper. Spread them around the chicken and return the pot to your oven.

Roast until the bird's skin is browned and the flesh is cooked through, about 20 minutes. To test for doneness, poke the leg near the socket. If the liquid runs pink, the chicken needs more time. If it runs clear, the chicken is ready.

Transfer the chicken, breast-side up, to a cutting board to rest for 30 minutes. This is important: if you cut into the meat without allowing it to rest, it won't be as juicy.

If your vegetables need more time, return the pan to your oven and roast until they're cooked through. Transfer the vegetables to a serving bowl and set aside. Pour any liquid remaining into a bowl to reserve. To make the jus, return the pan to the stove on high heat. Add the white wine and use a spoon to scrape up the brown bits that have stuck to the bottom of the pan. Add the reserved chicken liquid and stir until it comes to a simmer. Add salt to taste.

Once the chicken has rested, flip it onto its stomach and pull out the two small meat pockets around the middle of its back (you should be able to pull them out fairly easily using your hands). This is the "oyster"—or the best part of the chicken. Give one to your favorite guest and eat the other while you finish cutting the bird.

Flip the chicken onto its back and use a sharp knife to cut off the wings at the elbow. Cut a diagonal slice at each leg so they spread open, and pop each leg out of its joint using your thumb. Once the bone is free, cut the remaining skin and flesh to detach each leg.

Cut just to the right of the center breastbone, and then into the right side of the breast, meeting the middle slice so the meat easily falls off the bone. Repeat with the left breast. Cut off the wishbone by slicing across and down the breast, a few inches below the neck. Slice off the last part of the wing, and pull or cut off any pieces of meat that are left. Discard the stuffing (it's unsafe to eat) and return the carcass to the pot to make chicken stock (page 32).

Serve the jus in a separate bowl for dipping. Serve the roast chicken and vegetables together, family style.

Pairs well with *"Listen Here" by Eddie Harris*

Belgian Endive Gratin

Serves 6 to 8

2 cups whole milk

¼ cup butter, softened

3 tablespoons all-purpose flour

Salt and freshly ground black pepper

8 Belgian endives

Juice of 1 lemon

8 slices boiled deli ham

2 cups grated Gruyère cheese

It helps to know: This recipe requires an 8 by 12-inch gratin dish.

I first had this dish when it was served as a staff meal at a restaurant in France, and it has stuck with me all these years. I love it either as a side dish or a main course for a casual dinner party. It's an easy hit: it's hard to argue with ham and cheese.

To make a béchamel sauce, bring the milk to a simmer in a small pot on low heat. In a second small pot on low heat, melt 2 tablespoons of the butter. Add the flour to the butter to make a roux, whisking continuously to prevent it from burning. Continue whisking until the roux turns a light yellow color, about 10 minutes.

Slowly pour the simmering milk into the roux, a couple of tablespoons at a time. Whisk continuously on low heat until it thickens to a syrupy consistency. Season with a couple generous pinches each of salt and pepper. Remove the pan from the heat and set aside.

To prepare the endives, peel off the outer leaves until you're left with the firm and mostly white hearts. Trim and discard the bottom stem, being careful not to trim too high or they'll fall apart.

Melt the remaining 2 tablespoons butter in a large pot on medium heat. Working in batches, set the endives in the melted butter and turn until they're fully browned on each side, about 10 minutes total. Set the browned endives aside as you brown the remaining endives.

Preheat your oven to 375°F.

Return the endives to the pan. Turn the heat to low and add the lemon juice, 3 tablespoons water, and a pinch of salt. Cover the pan with the lid slightly ajar to allow steam to escape, and simmer until the endives are cooked through, about 20 minutes. Transfer to a plate and set aside to cool to room temperature.

Roll each endive in a ham slice like a blanket.

Whisk out any lumps from your béchamel, then spread a spoonful evenly across the bottom of your gratin dish. Set the ham-wrapped endives in one layer on top of the béchamel. Scoop the rest of the béchamel on top, then top with the Gruyère. Place the dish on a baking sheet to save you from a mess if it bubbles over. Bake until everything is heated through, caramelized, and bubbly, about 45 minutes. Serve immediately.

Pairs well with "Emotional Rescue" by The Rolling Stones

Lentil Soup with Smoked Ham

Serves 6 to 8

STOCK

2 smoked ham hocks

1 large leek, trimmed, white and tender green parts cut into large pieces

1 carrot, peeled and halved horizontally

1 rib celery, halved horizontally

1 head garlic, halved, skin on

2 black peppercorns

4 sprigs thyme

1 pound green or black lentils, rinsed in cold water

2 tablespoons extra-virgin olive oil, plus more for drizzling

Garlicky Herbed Croutons (page 26) (optional)

This dish is cured, smoked, and porky—everything one needs in a hearty winter soup. Making the stock with smoked ham hocks yields the best flavor for the lentils if you have the time. That said, you could also use 6 cups of any store-bought stock of your choice (or even water) and 8 ounces of cooked bacon in a pinch.

Put the ham hocks in a large pot on high heat, cover with water, and bring to a simmer. Once simmering, drain the water and return the hocks to the pot. This removes some of the salt from the ham hocks (don't skip this step or the soup will be too salty).

Cover the ham hocks with cold water and bring to a simmer on high heat. Once the water is simmering, turn the heat to low and add the leek, carrot, celery, garlic, peppercorns, and thyme. Cover the pot with the lid slightly ajar to allow steam to escape, and simmer until the ham hocks are tender, about 2½ hours.

Using tongs, transfer the ham hocks to a cutting board. Using a fine-mesh strainer, strain the remaining liquid over a large bowl, reserving the stock and discarding the vegetables and herbs. Peel off the skin and excess fat from the ham hocks and discard. Slice the remaining meat into bite-size pieces and set aside.

Return the pot to the stove on medium heat. Add the lentils, olive oil, and enough stock to cover the lentils by 2 inches. Bring to a simmer, turn the heat to medium-low, and cover the pot with the lid slightly ajar to allow steam to escape. Simmer for 20 minutes, then stir in the ham, cover as before, and simmer until the lentils are cooked through, about 40 minutes more.

To serve, ladle the soup into bowls and top each with a drizzle of olive oil and a handful of croutons.

Pairs well with "Louisiana Blues" by Muddy Waters

Ratatouille, Hot or Cold, Poached Egg or Not

Serves 6 to 8

1 pound white onions, quartered

1 pound red bell peppers

1 pound zucchini

1 large globe eggplant

4 large tomatoes (Early Girl or Roma preferred), peeled (see page 146)

¾ cup extra-virgin olive oil

8 cloves garlic, finely chopped

Espelette pepper or hot paprika

Salt

1 teaspoon fresh thyme leaves (from about 4 sprigs)

1 teaspoon tomato paste (optional)

2 tablespoons chopped fresh flat-leaf parsley leaves

2 tablespoons chopped basil leaves

Freshly ground black pepper

Poached eggs (see page 112) (optional)

This vegetable stew has been around for ages, yet feels as contemporary now as ever before. Though it's usually served hot as an accompaniment to a main protein, I love ratatouille cold, topped with a poached egg, as a refreshing main course in the summer when Provençal vegetables are at the height of seasonality.

I prefer to make this in a wide, heavy pot to allow for maximum evaporation and consolidation of flavor. Never let the stew sit on a boil; simmer it gently to ensure the vegetables maintain their shape. The extra step of reducing the vegetables' juices is well worth the added few minutes. If you have a big enough pot, double the recipe, as this keeps well for several days. In fact, this is one of those dishes that will taste better on the second day.

For the vegetables to cook at a similar rate, they must be cut to about the same size. Using the quartered onions as a reference point, prepare the bell peppers. Discard their stems and seeds, cut in half lengthwise, then cut again lengthwise to match the size of the onions.

The same applies to the zucchini and eggplant. Discard the ends, cut in half lengthwise, and cut to match the size of the onions, leaving the seeds in. Set aside in separate piles, as you'll cook them separately.

Cut the tomatoes in half horizontally. Squeeze their seeds out over the sink to discard and coarsely chop the remaining flesh. Set aside.

In a large pot on medium heat, combine the onions and ¼ cup of the olive oil, and sauté, stirring occasionally, so they soften but don't brown, about 10 minutes.

Add the bell peppers, garlic, a pinch of espelette pepper, and a large pinch of salt. Continue to cook until the bell peppers have softened. Transfer the onion and pepper mixture to a large bowl and set aside.

With the pot still on medium heat, stir together ¼ cup of the olive oil and the eggplant. Cook, stirring occasionally, until the eggplant begins to take on some color, about 2 minutes. Add the zucchini and cook until softened, about 4 minutes. Return the onion and pepper mixture to the pot and stir in the tomatoes and thyme until combined.

continued

At this point, the tomatoes will expel their water and the mixture will resemble a soup. Increase the heat until the liquid comes to a gentle boil, stirring occasionally to prevent sticking, then turn the heat to low and cover your pot with the lid slightly ajar to allow steam to escape. Simmer, stirring occasionally, until the vegetables are cooked through but maintain their shape, 1 to 1½ hours. Be careful to stir gently so as not to break up the vegetables.

Set a colander over a large bowl. Carefully transfer the entire contents of the pot into the colander, reserving both the vegetables and their juices.

Return the juices to the pot. Stir in the tomato paste and turn the heat to high. Bring the liquid to a boil, stirring often, until it has a thick and syrupy texture, 3 to 5 minutes.

Remove the pot from the heat and gently stir in the vegetables, parsley, basil, and the remaining ¼ cup olive oil, being careful not to break up the vegetables. Add salt and black pepper to taste.

Serve immediately on its own or topped with a poached egg, or chill the ratatouille thoroughly in your refrigerator before serving. Stored in an airtight container, the stew will keep in your refrigerator for up to 4 days.

Pairs well with "Bra" by Cymande

Spring Peas in a Casserole

Serves 4 to 6 as a side

1 clove garlic, halved

3 tablespoons butter, softened

1 head oak leaf or Bibb lettuce

2 cups shelled English peas

6 tender mint leaves

Salt

It helps to know: This recipe requires a small (about 5 by 6 inches) stovetop-safe casserole dish with a tight-fitting lid.

Peas à la française sounds fancy, but it's easy to make—shelling the peas being the most time-consuming part. From there, this side dish almost makes itself with a small amount of attention. In my mind, there's no better way to capture that fleeting, mythical spring pea moment than with this method.

Rub the cut side of the garlic clove over the bottom and sides of the casserole dish, then do the same with half of the butter.

Tear the lettuce leaves apart and press half of them into the sides and bottom of the casserole dish, overlapping to form a "bowl" (they don't need to be perfectly aligned). This makes a compartment to hold the peas.

In a small bowl, toss the peas with the mint leaves and a pinch of salt. Spoon the pea and mint mixture into the lettuce bowl. Dot the remaining 1½ tablespoons butter evenly on top of the peas by pinching off pieces about the size of a hazelnut. Pour 1 tablespoon water over the peas. Lay the rest of the lettuce on top of the peas to completely enclose them. Cover the casserole dish and place it on the stove on low heat.

This next part is magical. Be patient, as it requires a little bit of time. After 15 to 18 minutes, the butter will melt, the lettuce will release its water, and the peas will slowly stew in the butter-lettuce juices; it's sublime. Don't be afraid to take a peek! The dish is ready when its volume has reduced, liquid has formed in the pot, the lettuce has wilted, and the peas have turned an olive green.

Take the entire casserole dish to the table. Remove the lid and take a moment to appreciate the aroma. Serve immediately.

Pairs well with *"Ballade de Melody Nelson" by Serge Gainsbourg*

Chickpea Minestrone, Genovese Style

Serves 6 to 8

12 cups Chickpea Stock (page 34),
  Chicken Stock (page 32), or water

¼ cup extra-virgin olive oil

1 bunch spinach, coarsely chopped

1 bunch Swiss chard, thick stems
  discarded and leaves coarsely
  chopped

1 bunch Tuscan kale, thick stems
  discarded and leaves coarsely
  chopped

2 small zucchini, cut into ¼-inch slices

2 medium Yukon gold potatoes,
  cut into ½-inch slices

2 small Japanese eggplants
  or 1 globe eggplant, peeled,
  quartered, and cut into
  1-inch pieces

1 baseball-size turnip, peeled,
  quartered, and cut into ¼-inch slices

¾ cup macaroni

2 cups cooked chickpeas, or
  1 (15-ounce) can chickpeas, rinsed
  and drained

3 tablespoons Seven-Ingredient
  Pesto (page 22)

Salt and freshly ground black pepper

1 lemon wedge

Freshly grated Parmigiano-Reggiano
  for serving

I like to think of this recipe as more of a guide than a hard-and-fast rule. This minestrone is meant to be a pantry soup: throw in whatever you have on hand or whatever vegetables you like most. Maybe substitute rice for the macaroni or add a handful of mushrooms or other hearty greens. What makes this soup special is my ultimate pantry staple: a Genovese-style pesto. In the final moments, stir in the pesto and a squeeze of lemon, and what was once a basic pantry soup becomes a flavorful and healthy meal you can eat all week long.

In a large pot on high heat, bring the stock and olive oil to a boil. Add the spinach, chard, kale, zucchini, potatoes, eggplant, and turnip and turn the heat to low to maintain a gentle simmer. Cook, uncovered, for 1 hour.

Add the macaroni and simmer for 20 minutes. (The macaroni is overcooked on purpose, as the starch it releases gives the soup a nice texture.)

Add the chickpeas and simmer for 5 minutes. Stir in the pesto. Season with salt, pepper, and a squeeze of lemon to taste.

Ladle the minestrone into bowls. Serve with a bowl of freshly grated Parmigiano-Reggiano on the side.

Pairs well with *"Down Home Girl" by The Rolling Stones*

Cavolo Nero Gratin

Serves 2 to 4 as a main,
4 to 6 as a side

Butter for coating

Salt

2 bunches cavolo nero (Lacinato or
Tuscan kale), tough stems discarded

1 (15-ounce) can cannellini beans,
drained

1 clove garlic, finely chopped

½ teaspoon freshly ground
black pepper

Cayenne pepper

¾ cup crème fraîche

2 ounces Gruyère cheese,
finely grated

1 tablespoon untoasted dried
bread crumbs

It helps to know: **This recipe
requires an 8 by 12-inch
gratin dish.**

If I'm going to convince you to buy anything for your kitchen
(other than a $10 scale; see page 57), I hope it's a gratin dish. It's
an amazing investment that will make you a more versatile cook,
as you can "gratin" just about anything. Just pour some oil and/
or cream over leftover vegetables, meat, or fish; top with bread
crumbs and grated cheese; bake it in the oven; and voilà!, it's
a gratin. This one in particular takes kale and a can of beans and
makes a near-certain crowd-pleaser for any group. The hero
is most likely the crème fraîche, but the gratin dish helps, too
(I promise, it's worth it).

Preheat your oven to 425°F. Coat your gratin dish with butter.

Bring a large pot of water to a boil on high heat. Once boiling, add a pinch
of salt. Dunk the kale in the boiling water for 2 minutes to blanch. Drain and
cool on a cutting board. Shake out any excess water and coarsely chop into
bite-size pieces.

In a large mixing bowl, stir together the kale, beans, garlic, black pepper,
and a pinch each of cayenne and salt until combined. Spread the mixture
across the bottom of the gratin dish. Scoop the crème fraîche into even
dollops on top of the kale. Top with the Gruyère, then sprinkle on the bread
crumbs. Bake until the kale is soft and the Gruyère is brown and bubbly,
about 30 minutes.

Remove the dish from your oven and let the gratin rest for 10 minutes
before serving.

Pairs well with *"Ride Me High" by J. J. Cale*

Vegetable "Tart" with Saffron Mayonnaise

Serves 4 to 6 as a side

"TART"

2 tablespoons extra-virgin olive oil, plus more for drizzling

2 medium white onions, thinly sliced

2 cloves garlic, finely chopped

1 teaspoon fresh thyme leaves

2 tomatoes (Early Girl or Roma preferred), thinly sliced

1 medium zucchini, thinly sliced

1 small Japanese eggplant, thinly sliced

Salt

1 cup finely grated Parmigiano-Reggiano

SAFFRON MAYO (OPTIONAL)

½ teaspoon Spanish saffron threads

Mother-Sauce Mayo (page 17)

Juice of 1 lemon

It helps to know: This recipe requires an 8- to 9-inch baking dish. If you don't have a dish that large, you can use two small pie pans or halve the recipe.

This dish is the French interpretation of İmam bayıldı, a traditional Turkish stuffed eggplant. To me, it's the best of both worlds. One thing I love about this tart is that the "crust" is simply made of onions: there's no rolling or weighing involved. The layered vegetables are gloriously caramelized, not to mention just as pretty as a more traditional tart.

To make the "tart," in a large pan on medium heat, stir together the olive oil, onions, garlic, and thyme. Cook, stirring occasionally, until the onions are soft and lightly caramelized, about 20 minutes. Set aside to cool to room temperature.

Preheat your oven to 375°F.

Spread the onion mixture over the bottom of your baking dish to form a "crust." Layer the tomatoes, zucchini, and eggplant in a cascading circle on top of the onions. Alternate between the vegetables starting at the outside and working your way to the center. It can be as pretty or as haphazard as you want, as long as the vegetables remain in one layer.

Drizzle the surface with olive oil, top with a couple large pinches of salt, and bake until the top is nicely browned and caramelized, about 45 minutes.

Meanwhile, to make the mayo, lightly toast the saffron in a small, dry pan on medium heat, shaking the pan until the saffron becomes fragrant and starts to lightly brown, about 1 minute. Remove the pan from the heat and add 2 tablespoons water. The pan will sizzle and the water will turn a vibrant orange. Let cool to room temperature, then whisk the saffron water into your mayo, and stir in lemon juice to taste.

Remove the dish from your oven and let cool to room temperature.

Top with the grated Parmigiano-Reggiano and carve into slices like a pie. Serve the slices on their own or with the saffron mayo on the side.

Pairs well with "The Most Beautiful Girl" by Charlie Rich

Whole Roast Cauliflower with Capers & Egg

Serves 4 to 6 as a side, 2 as a main

6 anchovy fillets (salt-packed
   or oil-packed)

2 tablespoons capers

¼ cup dried bread crumbs

¾ cups extra-virgin olive oil,
   plus more for drizzling

1 large head cauliflower, trimmed

3 cloves garlic

Zest and juice of 1 lemon

Salt

1 egg, hard-boiled (see page 113)

2 tablespoons chopped fresh flat-leaf
   parsley leaves

This is a pescatarian version of an old trick in which I push anchovies into legs of lamb to flavor the meat as it roasts. Because the cauliflower is roasted whole, it's a bit showy, like a piece of roast meat, and perfect for a vegetable-focused meal that feels celebratory. Serve this on its own as a dinner for two, or alongside a simple green salad for a healthy meal to share.

Preheat your oven to 400°F.

In a fine-mesh strainer, rinse the anchovies and capers in cold water, then soak them covered with cold water in a small bowl for 10 minutes to remove their salt. Drain and set aside.

In a medium pan on low heat, fry the bread crumbs with ¼ cup of the olive oil, stirring frequently until they turn golden brown, 5 to 7 minutes. Drain using a fine-mesh strainer and spread onto a paper towel. Set aside.

Use a small knife to cut six small rectangular slots into the cauliflower, just large enough to fit a folded anchovy fillet. Spread the slices evenly on the upper half of the cauliflower. Fold the anchovies in half and use a small knife to stick them into their slots.

Thinly slice 1 garlic clove. Cut small slots across the cauliflower just large enough to hold the slices, and push the garlic slices into their slots.

Set the cauliflower in a medium ovenproof pan and coat with the remaining ½ cup olive oil. Place the remaining two garlic cloves next to the cauliflower. Top with the capers, lemon juice, and a pinch of salt. Add ⅓ cup water to the bottom of the pan and bake for 10 minutes.

Remove the pan from your oven and tilt it toward you, allowing the water and olive oil to pool at the bottom. Scoop the liquid over the cauliflower, basting it. Return the pan to your oven, continuing to baste the cauliflower every 10 to 15 minutes, until it has browned and cooked through, 45 minutes to 1 hour in total.

Remove the pan from your oven and transfer the cauliflower to your serving dish. Top with a drizzle of olive oil and any scrapings from the pan, then let cool to room temperature.

Finely grate the egg over the top of the cauliflower. Sprinkle with the lemon zest, bread crumbs, and parsley. Slice the cauliflower into slabs and serve immediately.

Pairs well with "Always Crashing in the Same Car" by David Bowie

Kale, Catalan Style

Serves 4 as a side

2 tablespoons golden raisins

2 tablespoons brandy

Salt

3 bunches Tuscan kale, thick bottom
stems discarded

2 ounces jamón Ibérico, prosciutto,
or bacon, cut into thin strips

2 tablespoons extra-virgin olive oil

1 Granny Smith apple, peeled and
finely diced

2 tablespoons pine nuts

¼ teaspoon red pepper flakes

Featuring raisins, pine nuts, and cooked greens, this is my take
on a Catalan dish that's traditionally made with spinach. I soak
the raisins in brandy and add apples and ham, giving this an
extra sweet-and-salty-and-boozy kick. The hearty kale is cooked
through, making it nicely soft and savory. Serve this alongside
grilled fish for a lighter meal or my Roast Chicken (page 202) for
a meal that's extra comforting.

In a small bowl, soak the raisins in the brandy and 2 tablespoons water
for 2 hours. Drain and set aside.

Bring a large pot of water to a simmer on high heat and set a bowl of ice
water next to your stove. Once boiling, add a pinch of salt. Blanch the kale
by submerging it in the simmering water for 2 minutes, then immediately
transfer it to the ice water to stop it from cooking further. Squeeze out the
water, pat the kale dry, and cut it horizontally into 2-inch-wide strips.

In a medium pan on low heat, stir together the ham and 1 tablespoon of
the olive oil until the meat is crispy, about 4 minutes.

Turn the heat to medium. Add the apple and pine nuts and cook, stirring
frequently, until the pine nuts have begun to take on some color, about
3 minutes. Stir in the raisins, kale, red pepper flakes, the remaining
1 tablespoon olive oil, and a couple pinches of salt. Continue to cook,
stirring frequently, until the kale has softened and takes on some of
the sweet flavor of the apple and raisins, 7 to 10 minutes.

Serve immediately, or at room temperature up to 1 hour later.

Pairs well with "Red Car" by Art Pepper

The Ultimate Potato Gratin

Serves 8 to 10 as a side

3 cups heavy whipping cream

3 cloves garlic, crushed

2 tablespoons salt

1 tablespoon freshly ground
   black pepper

4 tablespoons butter, softened

7 russet potatoes, peeled, rinsed,
   and cut into ¼-inch slices

1 cup grated Gruyère cheese

I call this the *ultimate* potato gratin because it's that rare baked potato dish that I consider to be a showstopper, especially as a hearty side to roasted meats in the fall and winter. With this method, salted cream infused with garlic soaks into the potatoes as they bake. As if that's not enough, it's topped with a layer of Gruyère cheese, which bubbles and browns to form a decadent crust. My advice: don't soak the potatoes in water—you need their starch to thicken the sauce.

Preheat your oven to 375°F.

In a medium pot on medium heat, combine the cream, garlic, salt, and pepper and bring to a simmer, stirring occasionally. Taste the cream every few minutes until it transforms from tasting very salty to tasting strongly of garlic, about 10 minutes. Strain over a large bowl. Discard the garlic and set the bowl of infused cream aside. Don't be alarmed if the cream tastes far too salty at this point; the potatoes will soak up the salt as they bake.

Coat the bottom and sides of your baking dish with 2 tablespoons of the butter, then cover the bottom with a thin layer of infused cream. Spread a layer of potatoes on top of the cream, overlapping the slices to resemble shingles. Add just enough cream to cover the potatoes. Continue this process, adding layers of cream, then potatoes, then cream, then potatoes, until you've filled your gratin dish (you may not use all of the potato slices).

Dot the surface of the dish with the remaining 2 tablespoons butter, placing small pieces of butter evenly across the top. Cover with aluminum foil, making sure the foil doesn't touch the surface of the potatoes. Use a knife to poke holes in the top to allow some steam to escape. Place the gratin dish on a baking sheet to save you from a mess in your oven if the cream bubbles over. Bake for 45 minutes. Remove the foil and bake until the surface starts to brown, about 20 minutes.

It helps to know: This recipe requires an 8 by 12-inch gratin dish.

Top with the Gruyère and bake until the cheese is melted and browned, about 10 minutes.

Remove the dish from your oven and let rest for 15 minutes before serving.

Pairs well with "Blue Train" by John Coltrane

Eggplant with Black Olive Tapenade

Serves 4 to 6

3 large globe eggplants, tops removed, thinly sliced lengthwise

Salt

½ cup capers

5 anchovy fillets (oil-packed)

1⅔ cups black olives (Greek or Niçoise preferred), pitted

2 cloves garlic, chopped

Freshly ground black pepper

Dried thyme, marjoram, or rosemary

4 to 5 tablespoons extra-virgin olive oil, plus more for brushing

It helps to know: **This recipe requires a food processor or blender.**

Eggplant is tragically underused in American kitchens. It's incredibly versatile, as shown in this dish, wherein the eggplant is simply baked and used as a base for tapenade, almost like a vegetable "tartine." I love to spoon this capery spread alongside fish, on toast, or on top of Smoky Eggplant "Caviar" (page 42)—name just about anything savory, and this tapenade will taste good scooped or spread or just spooned directly from your refrigerator with the door still half open (an act I usually reserve for ice cream). Feel free to make it ahead of time and store it in your refrigerator covered in olive oil for up to 2 weeks.

Sprinkle the eggplant slices with salt on both sides. Set aside for 30 minutes at room temperature to force out some of their water.

In a fine-mesh strainer, rinse the capers and anchovies in cold water, then soak them covered with cold water in a small bowl for 10 minutes to remove their salt. Drain and set aside.

Preheat your oven to 425°F and line a baking sheet with aluminum foil.

Meanwhile, in a food processor or blender, puree together the olives, capers, anchovies, garlic, and a pinch each of pepper and the dried herbs of your choice. With the food processor on low speed, slowly drizzle in the olive oil until it has fully incorporated and a paste has formed.

Pat the eggplants dry with a paper towel, then brush them with olive oil on each side. Place on the prepared baking sheet in a single layer. Bake for 15 minutes, flip, and bake until cooked through, about 15 minutes more.

Spread the olive tapenade on top of the eggplant slices and serve.

Pairs well with "The Seventh Son" by Mose Allison

NOT-TOO-SWEET, TO FINISH

Let's get this out of the way: I think dessert is fine. I like it, but I'm not crazy about it. I don't have a strong sweet tooth, so more often than not, I prefer to have a cheese course at the end of a meal, making cheese the obvious start to this chapter. In fact, when I'm in the mood for a lighter dinner, I might opt for a simple plate of fresh fruit as a final course. Finding a piece of fruit so extraordinary that it can be served by itself, especially after an ambitious meal, is an understated and elegant way to finish any dinner.

That said, for obvious reasons, I can't fill these pages with my favorite sliced fruit on a plate. And truly, I love each and every one of these desserts (almost) as much as fresh seasonal fruit at the peak of ripeness. That's because these recipes aren't too sweet. What's more, many of these dishes—like the Lemon Caramel (page 244)—give me the chance to showcase one of my passions: all things citrus.

If I'm being honest, I had to resist writing "would be good with vanilla ice cream" for nearly every recipe in this chapter. Most of these dishes, like Strawberries in a Rosé Wine Hibiscus Syrup (page 233), are really meant as an accompaniment to my standard dessert of choice: store-bought vanilla ice cream. A tub of ice cream is also, conveniently, a low-pressure response to, "What should I bring?", so I encourage you to delegate on this one.

What I do cherish about dessert is its unique ability to bring out the inner child in all of us: sweets are meant to be fun. These dishes aren't an everyday pleasure, but rather an indulgence reserved for special occasions. It's your chance to be playful, as when picking the toppings for the Rice Pudding Sundae (page 242), or deciding what "kind" of butter to use in the Special Butter Cake (page 249). Anything that requires rolling, like the Day-After Meyer Lemon Tart (page 234), or freezing, like the Almond Granita (page 262), can be made in advance. Dessert signals that the end of the night is approaching. You're likely a few glasses in, and it's your time to relax, so I wrote these recipes to allow you to do just that.

So, if it's summertime, and you've planned a whole meal for your closest friends using recipes exclusively from this book (smart of you), and you found the most perfect melon at the farmers' market, feel free to skip this chapter altogether. But if you're looking for something not-too-sweet, or something creamy and fatty and savory (depending on the cheese), the following recipes are desserts that hold their own against something no chef can match: the profound pleasure of a ripe fruit, or the humble decadence of a scoop of store-bought vanilla ice cream.

How to Build a Cheese Course

I'll take fat over sugar as a general rule, so to me, cheese is the ultimate dessert. I don't think this is an unpopular opinion: nearly everyone loves cheese. Rather than serve it at the beginning of the meal, consider saving the best for last. It's my favorite way to finish a dinner party because you can keep drinking the wine that's already open and enjoy yourself with little effort. Plus, if ease is your endgame, this is the one page in the book where I'll encourage you not to cook. Building a cheese plate only requires yet another thing I love: shopping.

When I go to a restaurant, I don't claim to know everything about wine and exactly what I want to order. I have conversations with the sommeliers, who spend their entire careers building their list. I'm not shy about telling them what I like, that I don't want to spend a fortune, and asking about the wine they're excited about at the moment. In other words, I delegate. Cheese is no different. Whether it's a sommelier, a cheesemonger, a butcher, or the farmer selling produce at the market, someone who cares deeply about what they do will be happy when you show an interest, and more importantly, humility and a desire to learn. You'll benefit from their knowledge in the end.

If you're building a cheese plate, the first step is to find a local cheese shop. Hopefully you live near a shop with a knowledgeable and passionate staff. Tell them how many guests you're expecting and when they're coming over. This will give them an idea of how much cheese you need, and how the cheese will taste when it's served. Finally, tell them that you want a sheep, a cow, and a goat cheese. From there, your final choices should be some combination of both hard and soft. Maybe a soft cow, hard sheep, and goat somewhere in between. Or a soft goat, hard cow, and an in-between sheep—you get the idea.

The best thing about shopping for cheese is that tasting is part of the process. Taste with the merchants, tell them what you like, narrow down to a few choices, then ask if there's anything in the shop that they're particularly thrilled about. Maybe throw in a fourth cheese if you find something interesting, or a fifth—you really can't go wrong with having leftover cheese.

For accompaniments, I like thin, crisp crackers with no herbs. Or, I just let my guests rip off fat pieces of baguette. Add something sweet, like fruit preserves or honey. Lightly toasted nuts, especially with a blue cheese, is also a lovely addition. In the end, remember that the beauty of a cheese course is in its simplicity—the whole point is to not stress. Like I said, everyone loves cheese.

Strawberries in a Rosé Wine Hibiscus Syrup

Serves 4

1 vanilla bean, or 1 teaspoon
  vanilla extract

2 cups dry rosé wine

⅓ cup sugar

¼ cup dried hibiscus flowers

1 pound strawberries, washed and
  hulled (see page 71)

Softly whipped fresh cream or vanilla
  ice cream for serving (optional)

These strawberries are tart and floral, and, like most dishes in this chapter, go very well with vanilla ice cream. If you've ever had a Jamaica, the iced tea drink made from hibiscus flowers, you know that the syrup will be an intensely vivid maroon-pink. The syrup combined with simple ripe fresh fruit is everything I want in a dessert at home: tasty, fun, simple, sweet-but-not-too-sweet, and, best of all, pretty.

To separate the vanilla bean from its pod, split the pod in half lengthwise. Use a small knife to scrape out the seeds, then wipe them on the side of the pod. This is the easiest, cleanest way to utilize both the seeds and pod.

In a medium pot on high heat, bring the wine and sugar to a boil. Once boiling, turn the heat to low and simmer, stirring occasionally, until the sugar has dissolved and the majority of the alcohol has cooked out, about 5 minutes.

Remove the pot from the heat and stir in the hibiscus flowers and vanilla bean (if you're using vanilla extract, don't add it yet). Let the wine cool to room temperature. It will infuse with the vanilla and hibiscus while it cools.

Strain the syrup over a large bowl, reserving the liquid that's formed. Use a large spoon to press as much liquid as possible from the hibiscus flowers. Discard the flowers and vanilla bean. If you're using vanilla extract, stir it into the syrup.

Quarter the larger strawberries and halve the smaller ones. Put them in a bowl large enough to hold both the strawberries and the syrup. Pour the rosé syrup over the strawberries. Cover and set in your refrigerator to chill for at least 30 minutes or up to 2 hours.

Divide the berries and a generous amount of syrup among four glasses. Serve as is, or with a spoonful of whipped cream or vanilla ice cream.

Pairs well with "I Feel Love" by Donna Summer

Day-After Meyer Lemon Tart

Serves 8 to 10

CRUST

250 grams butter, softened,
    plus 2 teaspoons for greasing

160 grams confectioners' sugar

2 eggs, at room temperature

370 grams all-purpose flour

100 grams cornstarch

5 grams salt

FILLING

12 Meyer lemons

8 eggs, at room temperature

2 cups granulated sugar, sifted
    (increase this by ¼ cup if you're
    using regular lemons)

¾ cup butter, softened

**It helps to know: This recipe
requires uncooked rice or dried
beans for weighting the crust.**

continued

When this tart sets, the flavors meld, and it tastes even better the next day, so it's the perfect dessert to prepare the night before a dinner party. It's one of the few recipes in this book where I'll make a case for buying a $10 digital scale. The volume of a cup of flour will differ on a sunny day versus a rainy day, enough to throw off the entire recipe. But 370 grams of flour is, and always will be, 370 grams of flour.

That said, if you're ready to turn to the next page because a scale is just too much, consider making only the filling instead. It's a simple lemon curd that's delicious on ice cream, yogurt, or toast in the morning; on its own; or perhaps with ricotta cheese.

First make the crust. (This is easily done by pulsing in a food processor, but since I already made you buy a scale, I'll explain it the low-tech way.) In a large bowl, cream together the butter and confectioners' sugar using a wooden spoon until well combined (it will look fluffy and lighter in color). Beat in one egg until fully incorporated. Repeat with the second egg. Sift in the flour, cornstarch, and salt and continue to beat until a dough has formed. Shape the dough into a ball and flatten it with the palm of your hand. Wrap in plastic and place in your refrigerator to chill for 1 hour.

Preheat your oven to 375°F. Grease a 9- to 11-inch tart mold with 2 teaspoons butter.

Remove the dough from your refrigerator and place it between a folded piece of parchment paper to prevent sticking. Roll the dough into a circle about ¼ inch thick and a bit larger than your tart mold. Carefully transfer the rolled-out dough to your buttered tart mold. Use your fingers to gently press the dough into the sides of the tart mold, then cut off any excess dough draping over the top—you want the crust to just come to the top of your mold. Use a fork to poke holes across the bottom of the tart shell to prevent it from puffing up as it bakes.

Line the shell with cheesecloth, draping it over the side of the mold to prevent the edges from burning. Fill the cheesecloth with a ½-inch layer of uncooked rice or dried beans to make a weight that prevents the dough from puffing. Return the dough to your refrigerator to chill until firm, about 5 minutes.

Bake until the shell is nicely browned around the edges, about 25 minutes. Remove and discard the weights and cheesecloth and continue to bake until the middle is browned, about 5 minutes more. Remove the crust from your oven and set aside to cool.

To make the filling, grate the zest from the lemons into a large bowl. Juice the lemons into a separate bowl, then strain the juice into the bowl with the zest.

Whisk in the eggs and granulated sugar.

Pour the mixture into a saucepan on medium-low heat. Using a wooden spoon, stir constantly until the mixture begins to thicken. Never allow the mixture to boil or it will curdle. (If it does curdle, don't panic! Keep reducing it, add the butter, and then transfer it to a blender and blend until smooth.) Once the mixture has thickened considerably, 10 to 15 minutes, pour it into a large bowl. Stir in the butter, 1 tablespoon at a time, until all of the butter has been incorporated.

Pour the filling into your tart shell and let cool to room temperature to set the filling. Cover the tart with plastic wrap and chill in your refrigerator for at least 1 hour, or ideally overnight. Remove 10 minutes before serving. Leftovers can be stored, covered, in your refrigerator for up to 5 days.

Pairs well with *"Hanging on the Telephone" by Blondie*

Figs & Fennel

Serves 4 to 6

6 tablespoons honey

½ (750-ml) bottle sweet dessert wine, such as a Sauternes or sweet Riesling

2 heads wild fennel, flowers and stems intact, or 2 fennel bulbs, outer layers discarded

½ teaspoon fennel seeds

10 slightly firm fresh figs

Vanilla ice cream for serving (optional)

Wild fennel grows like a weed in California. If you happen upon it—pick the flowering heads and tender shoots. They dry well and make a welcome addition to fish or just about anything on the grill. I love wild fennel for this dish, but if you can't find it, store-bought fennel bulbs also work. This recipe keeps well in your refrigerator, so feel free to make it in advance. Serve it on its own, or like most things, it's even better with vanilla ice cream.

In a medium pan on low heat, combine the honey, wine, fennel, and fennel seeds and bring to a simmer.

Meanwhile, use a toothpick to poke three holes around the base of each fig.

When the honey has melted and the wine is simmering, place the figs in the pan stem-side up and cover the pan with a tight-fitting lid. Poach until the figs are soft, about 8 minutes.

Transfer the figs to a bowl, reserving the liquid in the pan. Turn the heat to high and simmer until the wine mixture has reduced by half and has the consistency of syrup, about 8 minutes.

Pour the warm syrup over the figs, cover, and set in your refrigerator to chill for at least 30 minutes or up to 1 week.

Divide the figs among serving bowls, drizzling plenty of syrup on top. Serve as is, or with a scoop of vanilla ice cream.

Pairs well with *"Ngalam" by Orchestra Baobab*

Roasted Figs with Pomegranate

Seeds from 2 medium pomegranates

Juice from 1 orange

Juice from 1 lemon

½ cup dry red wine

6 black peppercorns (optional)

2 tablespoons butter

8 to 10 fresh figs, halved

Figs have two seasons: a quick burst in early summer and a longer run in the fall. This dessert is best for the second crop in the fall when both figs and pomegranates are delightfully ripe. Perfect for those of us who aren't really dessert people, this dish is low-maintenance, spicy, citrusy, and winey, and it combines fresh fruit and cooked fruit in all the best ways.

Preheat your oven to 375°F.

Lightly crush half of the pomegranate seeds in a large bowl to release their juices. Stir in the orange and lemon juices, the red wine, and peppercorns.

In a medium pot over medium heat, melt the butter until it foams and begins to lightly brown. Add the pomegranate seed mixture and stir for 30 seconds. Remove the pot from the heat and set aside.

Arrange the figs in a single layer in a baking dish, cut-side up. Pour the butter and pomegranate mixture over the figs. Roast, removing the dish every 5 minutes or so to baste (scoop the juices pooled at the bottom over the top of the figs), until the figs are softened but maintain their shape, about 18 minutes. Remove the dish from your oven and let cool for 5 minutes.

To serve, sprinkle the figs with the remaining pomegranate seeds. Divide among serving bowls, scooping plenty of juice and pomegranate seeds over the top.

Pairs well with "The Pusher" by Nina Simone

Rice Pudding Sundae

Serves 4 to 6

1 vanilla bean, or 1 teaspoon
  vanilla extract

2½ cups whole milk

½ cup short-grain white rice

Salt

3 tablespoons sugar

1 cup heavy whipping cream

Toppings of your choice

This lighthearted, fun, and quick dessert is the perfect way to bring out your guests' inner child. Give everyone their own bowl of rice pudding and set up the assorted toppings like a sundae bar in the center of the table. Imagine how you would top an adult ice cream sundae: fresh fruit, nuts, granola, praline, dried fruit, trail mix, or my favorite, Lemon Caramel (page 244). I'm not a huge fan of cinnamon myself, but you can add it if you like. Nutmeg is also a welcome addition, as long as it's freshly grated.

To separate the vanilla bean from its pod, split the pod in half lengthwise. Use a small knife to scrape out the seeds, then wipe them on the side of the pod. This is the easiest, cleanest way to utilize both the seeds and pod.

In a medium pot on medium heat, combine the milk, vanilla bean or extract, rice, and a pinch of salt and bring to a simmer. Cook, stirring frequently, until the rice is soft and slightly overcooked, 25 to 30 minutes. Turn down the heat if the milk starts to bubble and boil over, and stir from the bottom of the pot to prevent the rice from sticking.

When the rice is cooked through and resembles a porridge, stir in the sugar and remove the pot from the stove. Pour the rice into a large serving bowl and let cool to room temperature.

Meanwhile, whip the cream until it forms soft peaks. In other words, when you lift the whisk up, the cream holds a peak for a second or two, but quickly melts back into itself.

When the rice pudding has cooled, remove the vanilla bean and fold in the whipped cream. Ladle into bowls and serve with the toppings of your choice.

Pairs well with "Shoo Ra" by Dr. John

Lemon Caramel

Makes about 1 cup

1 vanilla bean, or 1 teaspoon vanilla
 extract

1 cup sugar

¾ cup heavy whipping cream

Juice from 2 small lemons

Salt

Caramel is the one sweet that I just can't turn down—I absolutely adore the flavor of burnt sugar. This caramel combines burnt sugar with my other great food obsession: citrus. It's everything I could ask for in a sauce. Serve this with the Rice Pudding Sundae (page 242), or over yogurt or vanilla ice cream, perhaps topped with a spoonful of salty granola.

To separate the vanilla bean from its pod, split the pod in half lengthwise. Use a small knife to scrape out the seeds, then wipe them on the side of the pod. This is the easiest, cleanest way to utilize both the seeds and pod.

Pour ½ cup water into a small pot on low heat. Carefully pour the sugar into the center of the pot (you don't want the sugar to touch the sides or it will crystallize). Without stirring, turn the heat to high. Continue to watch the pot, without stirring, until the sugar melts, the water evaporates, and the liquid turns a light golden straw color, about 9 minutes.

Turn the heat to medium and watch carefully while the sugar turns a medium to dark amber (in other words, the color of caramel), 2 to 3 minutes more.

Meanwhile, warm the cream in a small pan on low heat or in a bowl in your microwave. This will reduce the amount of sputtering and splashing when you add it to the hot sugar.

Turn off the heat under the caramel, leaving the pot on the burner. Pour in a small splash of cream at a time. (Be careful, it will sputter and spit.) Swirl the pan to mix. When it stops sputtering, add another splash of cream. Continue with this process until you've added all of the cream.

Remove the pan from the burner and stir in the vanilla bean or extract, the lemon juice, and a pinch of salt. Set aside to cool to room temperature.

Remove the vanilla bean and use immediately, or store covered in your refrigerator for up to 2 weeks.

Pairs well with "Move It" by The Chantays

A Few Fresh Compotes

Serves 4 to 6

To compote is essentially to poach fruit in syrup, but unlike a jam, the fruit is not preserved. In order to safely preserve fruit to be used year-round, jams require a high amount of sugar. The beauty of a compote is that you can cook a ripe fruit without adding much sugar and enjoy its natural flavors right away, preferably while still warm, and especially with vanilla ice cream.

A Mixed Berry Compote

2 cups mixed berries (blackberries, raspberries, sliced strawberries, and so on)

2 tablespoons sugar

In a bowl, stir together the berries and sugar. Pour the mixture into a pot and set over low heat. Stir gently until the fruit begins to release its juices, about 2 minutes. After the mixture starts to bubble and break down into liquid, simmer gently for 5 minutes, stirring occasionally. Serve warm.

A Cherry Compote with Lemon Verbena

2 cups sweet cherries, halved and pitted

½ cup sugar

5 lemon verbena leaves

In a small pot, combine the cherries and sugar. Add ¼ cup water and the lemon verbena. Set the pot over low heat and stir occasionally until the mixture comes to a simmer. Simmer until the cherries are completely soft, 6 to 8 minutes. Remove the pot from the heat and discard the lemon verbena. Serve warm.

continued

A Stone Fruit & Basil Compote with Mascarpone Cream

MASCARPONE CREAM

2 eggs, separated

3 tablespoons sugar

8 ounces mascarpone cheese

1 tablespoon freshly squeezed orange juice

Zest of 1 orange

COMPOTE

½ cup sugar

2 cups chopped apricots or peaches (4 to 6 medium peaches or apricots)

6 to 8 small basil leaves or large leaves halved with kitchen scissors

To make the mascarpone cream, in a large bowl, whisk together the egg yolks and sugar until creamy and pale in color. Add the mascarpone and whisk until just incorporated.

In a separate bowl, whisk the egg whites until stiff. In other words, when you lift the whisk, the egg whites hold their shape. Gently fold the egg whites into the egg yolk mixture along with the orange juice and zest. Cover the bowl with plastic wrap and place in your refrigerator to firm for at least 30 minutes or up to I hour.

Meanwhile, to make the compote, in a small pot over medium-high heat, stir together the sugar and ¾ cup water. Simmer, stirring frequently, until the sugar has dissolved, about 5 minutes. Add the fruit, bring the mixture back to a simmer, then turn the heat to low and simmer until the fruit is completely soft, 8 to 10 minutes. Remove the pot from the heat and stir in the basil to taste.

To serve, scoop the compote into bowls and add a dollop of mascarpone cream on top.

Pairs well with *"Cracking Up" by Nick Lowe*

→ Clockwise from top: A Stone Fruit & Basil Compote; A Cherry Compote with Lemon Verbena; Mascarpone Cream; A Mixed Berry Compote

Special Butter Cake

Serves 6

½ cup plus 1 tablespoon butter, softened, plus 2 teaspoons for greasing

½ cup plus 2 tablespoons sugar

2 large eggs

Zest and juice of 1 orange

Zest and juice of 1 lemon

1 cup all-purpose flour

1 tablespoon baking powder

Salt

This is a simple, rich, and moist cake for which you should choose your butter (and your friends) wisely. Easily made in California and a handful of other states, the number of which are increasing every four years or so, it's perhaps a dessert best enjoyed at the beginning of the meal. In the words of Alice B. Toklas describing the Haschich Fudge in her 1954 bestseller *The Alice B. Toklas Cook Book*: "This is the food of Paradise—of Baudelaire's *Artificial Paradises*: it might provide an entertaining refreshment for a Ladies' Bridge Club or a chapter meeting of the DAR. In Morocco it is thought to be good for warding off the common cold in damp winter weather and is, indeed, more effective if taken with large quantities of hot mint tea. Euphoria and brilliant storms of laughter; ecstatic reveries and extension of one's personality on several simultaneous planes are to be complacently expected."

Preheat your oven to 350°F. Grease a cake pan with 2 teaspoons butter. Sprinkle 2 tablespoons of the sugar into the pan, then shake and tilt the pan until it's evenly coated in the sugar. Turn the pan upside down and tap it to shake off any excess sugar.

In a large bowl, use a wooden spoon to stir together the remaining butter and sugar until combined. Add the eggs, one at a time, mixing each with the wooden spoon until thoroughly combined.

Grate the zest from the orange and lemon over the bowl and then add the juice (no need to strain). Mix until smooth.

Sift the flour, baking powder, and a pinch of salt into a small bowl and stir to combine. Fold the flour mixture into the batter and mix until just combined.

Pour the batter into the prepared cake pan and tap the pan gently on your countertop to settle the batter into an even layer. Bake until the cake starts to pull away from the sides of the pan and turn golden, about 25 minutes.

Remove the cake from your oven and let it cool until it's just slightly warm. Turn the cake out of the pan, cut it into thick slices, and serve.

It helps to know: This recipe requires a 9- to 10-inch round cake pan.

Pairs well with "High & Wild" by Angel Olsen

Rich Chocolate Cake with Sea Salt

Serves 6 to 8

115 grams butter, softened, plus
   2 teaspoons for greasing

50 grams all-purpose flour, sifted,
   plus 2 tablespoons for sprinkling

100 grams dark chocolate
   (at least 70 percent cacao)

50 grams milk chocolate

2 eggs

55 grams sugar

Kosher salt

Flaky sea salt

Softly whipped cream for
   serving (optional)

It helps to know: **This recipe
requires a scale and a 9 by
5-inch loaf pan.**

This recipe is best described as a chocolate pound cake—it's just as rich as it is delicate. The flaky salt sea brings out the flavor of the chocolate in a way that reminds me of salted caramel, my favorite combination of salty and sweet. Though you can make this dessert using a round cake pan, I prefer to use a loaf pan as an allusion to the pound cake. Feel free to make it up to a day in advance and reheat it just before serving.

Preheat your oven to 325°F. Bring a large pot of water to a simmer over high heat. Grease the bottom and sides of a loaf pan with 2 teaspoons of the butter. Sprinkle 2 tablespoons of the flour into the pan, then shake and tilt the pan until it's evenly coated in flour. Turn the pan upside down and tap it on the counter to remove any excess flour.

Combine the chocolate and the remaining 115 grams butter in a large heatproof bowl set over the simmering water. Stir until the chocolate has melted and combined with the butter.

In a large bowl, beat together the eggs and sugar until the mixture lightens in color. Add the remaining 50 grams flour and stir to combine. Add the melted chocolate mixture along with a pinch of kosher salt; mix until an even paste forms. Do your best not to overwork the batter or the cake will lose some of its density.

Pour the batter into the prepared cake pan. Set the pan on a baking sheet (which acts as a barrier from the heat and avoids a mess in your oven if the batter spills over). Bake until the cake starts to pull away from the edges of the pan, and the top is browned and caramelized, about 25 minutes.

Remove the cake from your oven and let it cool until it's just slightly warm. Turn the cake out of the pan and cut it into thick slices.

To serve, top each slice with a generous sprinkling of flaky sea salt and a dollop of whipped cream.

Pairs well with *"I Can Only Give You Everything" by Them*

Lost Bread with Apples

Serves 4

2 eggs plus 2 egg yolks

¾ cup whole milk

¼ cup dark rum

1 teaspoon ground cinnamon

¼ cup plus 1 tablespoon sugar

Salt

4 (1-inch-thick) slices stale levain

2 cups apple cider

10 tablespoons butter

½ teaspoon apple cider vinegar

1 Granny Smith apple, peeled, seeded, and cut into thin wedges

Vanilla ice cream or softly whipped cream for serving (optional)

Pain perdu, or French toast, literally translates to "lost bread," so named because you use dry bread that would normally be thrown away. The dry, firm bread soaks up the egg mixture without getting mushy. Far from lost, this toast is best served as a late-night dessert or even a (very) decadent breakfast. Sweet, yes, but also boozy, which strikes a good balance in my opinion.

In a bowl, whisk together the eggs, egg yolks, milk, rum, and cinnamon until combined. Whisk in the sugar and a pinch of salt. Pour the mixture into a rimmed baking sheet or casserole dish and lay the bread in the liquid. Set aside, flipping the bread every so often until it's soaked through, 30 minutes to 1 hour.

Place a cooling rack over your sink and set the bread on top. Allow any excess liquid to drip out of the bread.

Meanwhile, in a small pot on medium heat, reduce the apple cider to a syrupy consistency, swirling the pan every so often to prevent it from boiling, about 30 minutes. Whisk in 6 tablespoons of the butter, 1 tablespoon at a time, until melted and combined. Whisk in the apple cider vinegar. Set aside.

Preheat your oven to 325°F.

Melt 3 tablespoons of the butter in a large ovenproof pan on medium heat until it starts to sizzle and foam. Lay the bread slices in the pan and cook until they're nicely browned, 3 to 5 minutes. Flip and brown on the other side, 3 to 5 minutes more.

Place the pan in your oven and bake until the bread is crisped through, about 15 minutes. Transfer the bread to a wire rack to cool for 2 minutes.

Meanwhile, melt the remaining 1 tablespoon butter in a medium pan on medium-high heat. When the butter starts to foam, add the apple and cook, stirring and flipping often, until it caramelizes, about 10 minutes.

Divide the bread among serving plates or bowls and top with the caramelized apples. Drizzle on the apple syrup and serve with a scoop of vanilla ice cream or a dollop of whipped cream.

Pairs well with "Makin' Whoopee" by The Ben Webster Quintet

Almond & Oat Crisp with Mixed Berries

Serves 6

1½ pounds mixed berries (strawberries, raspberries, blackberries) or other sliced fruit

4 heaping tablespoons granulated sugar

1 tablespoon corn starch

Salt

1¼ cups all-purpose flour

7 tablespoons butter, softened or coarsely chopped

⅔ cup whole blanched almonds, finely chopped

¼ cup light brown sugar

¾ cup steel-cut oats

This is a wonderful way to use an abundance of fruit in the summertime. Choose one type of berry or keep things colorful by using a variety—I even throw in some sliced peaches when they look particularly enticing. Don't worry about buttering your baking dish: you'll find yourself scraping up every last bit of the stuck, gooey, caramelized fruit from its sides.

Preheat your oven to 350°F.

Wash and fully dry the berries. If using strawberries, wash and hull them (see page 71) and cut the larger ones in half. Toss the fruit in a bowl with the granulated sugar, corn starch, and a pinch of salt. Spread the berries in an even layer in a medium ovenproof dish.

In a large bowl, combine the flour and butter. Rub the mixture between your palms until the two combine to resemble coarse sand. Add the almonds, brown sugar, and oats and stir to combine. Sprinkle 2 to 3 tablespoons water over the crumble mixture and shake the bowl until the water adheres to the flour and larger pebbles start to form. Scatter the crumble mixture over the surface of the berries. Don't press down; you want to keep the mixture loose.

Bake the crisp until the top is golden and the fruit begins to bubble up to the surface, about 45 minutes. Serve warm.

Pairs well with *"Who Drove the Red Sports Car?" by Van Morrison*

Olallieberry Crumble

Serves 6

BASE

2 teaspoons butter for greasing

¼ cup granulated sugar, plus
 2 tablespoons for sprinkling

Zest of 2 lemons

2¼ tablespoons all-purpose flour

1½ tablespoons freshly squeezed
 lemon juice

4 cups olallieberries

CRUMBLE

½ cup butter, softened

⅔ cup light brown sugar

1½ cups all-purpose flour, sifted

½ teaspoon salt

¼ teaspoon baking soda

This old-fashioned crumble is homey, perhaps nostalgic, and incredibly easy to make. Serve it warm or at room temperature, on its own or with vanilla ice cream. This probably goes without saying, but it also makes a delicious breakfast the following day. Olallieberries are found at the farmers' markets in California in the summer months, but you can substitute blackberries, raspberries, strawberries, blueberries, or a combination of your choosing.

Preheat your oven to 350°F. Grease a large baking dish with the butter. Sprinkle the dish with 2 tablespoons of the granulated sugar, then shake and tilt the dish until it's evenly coated. Turn the pan upside down and tap it to shake off any excess sugar.

To make the base, stir together the remaining ¼ cup granulated sugar, the lemon zest, and flour. In a separate bowl, pour the lemon juice over the berries, then very carefully stir them into the sugar and flour mixture. Spread the fruit in a single layer in your prepared baking dish.

To make the crumble, in the bowl of a stand mixer fitted with the paddle attachment, cream together the butter and brown sugar. Alternatively, you can use a wooden spoon to beat the butter and sugar together until incorporated (but before "fluffy"). Scrape the bowl, then add the flour, salt, and baking soda and stir until a dough forms.

Crumble the dough between your fingers over the top of the fruit. Bake until the topping is brown and the berries are bubbling, about 25 minutes.

Serve warm.

Pairs well with "That Summer Feeling" by Jonathan Richman

Cherry Clafoutis

Serves 6

5 tablespoons butter, melted, plus 2 teaspoons for greasing

½ cup granulated sugar, plus 2 tablespoons for sprinkling

1 pound sweet cherries, stems removed

2 eggs

⅔ cup whole milk

¾ cup all-purpose flour

Vanilla extract (optional)

Confectioners' sugar for garnish

It helps to know: **This recipe requires an 8- or 9-inch baking dish.**

This is one of my all-time favorite traditional French desserts, especially for a long lunch party out on the deck. I've found that this clafoutis works best when the cherries are left intact (meaning, pits in). The juice comes out in the baking process and pitting them only results in mushy fruit. As an added bonus, not having to remove the cherry pits means this dessert is nearly effortless to make. Just be sure to alert your guests that the cherries have pits! This is also incredibly tasty with fresh sliced figs or apricots, so if you're lucky enough to find some that are nicely ripe, use them in place of or in addition to the cherries.

Preheat your oven to 350°F. Grease an 8-inch or 9-inch baking dish with 2 teaspoons of the butter. Sprinkle the dish with 2 tablespoons of the granulated sugar, then shake and tilt the dish until it's evenly coated. Turn the pan upside down and tap it to shake off any excess sugar.

Spread the cherries in a single layer in the prepared baking dish.

Beat the eggs and the remaining ½ cup granulated sugar together in a large bowl. Whisk in the milk and flour. Add the remaining 5 tablespoons melted butter and a couple of drops of vanilla extract and beat until combined.

Pour the batter evenly over the top of the cherries (don't worry if some of the cherries poke through the batter). Bake until the batter puffs up and begins to turn golden, about 30 minutes. To test for doneness, stick a toothpick into the center of the batter and make sure it comes out clean.

Remove the dish from your oven and dust the surface liberally with confectioners' sugar. Slice and serve warm straight from the oven, or let cool and serve at room temperature.

Pairs well with *"Le Temps de l'Amour" by Françoise Hardy*

Avery's Chocolate Chip Cookies

Makes about 10 large cookies

¾ cup butter, softened

1½ cups light brown sugar, sifted

2 large eggs

1 teaspoon vanilla extract

2½ cups whole-wheat flour, sifted

¾ teaspoon baking soda, sifted

Salt

1¾ cups dark chocolate chips (at least 55 percent cacao; I use Valrhona)

1½ cups walnuts, lightly toasted (see page 83) and chopped

Our friendship aside, Avery Ruzicka, the head baker and my partner at Manresa Bread, makes the best chocolate chip cookies I've ever eaten. If you don't have a stand mixer, you can use an electric hand mixer, just be sure to keep the speed low so as not to break up the walnut and chocolate pieces. The dough also bakes from frozen exceptionally well, so you can preemptively practice self-control and make yourself just a couple at a time. Simply form the dough into a log and store it, wrapped tightly, in your freezer for up to 1 month. When you find yourself in a freshly baked chocolate chip cookie kind of mood, slice off a disk or two of dough and bake them for a minute longer than called for below.

Preheat your oven to 350°F and line a baking sheet with parchment paper.

Combine the butter and brown sugar in the bowl of a stand mixer fitted with the paddle attachment. Mix on medium-low speed until just combined (not "light and fluffy"), 1 to 2 minutes.

With the speed still on medium-low, add the eggs and vanilla extract and mix until combined.

Turn the speed to low and add the flour. When the flour has been incorporated, add the baking soda and a pinch of salt. Scrape down the sides of the bowl and mix on low speed for 1 minute more to ensure the ingredients are fully combined.

With the speed still on low, add the chocolate, then the walnuts. Mix until just combined. Scrape down the sides of the bowl and check the bottom of the mixer to make sure all the dough is homogeneous.

Using a medium-size ice cream scoop, scoop the dough onto the prepared baking sheet. Press lightly on top of each ball to flatten it ever so slightly. (The cookies contain a high filling-to-flour ratio, and flattening the top helps maintain a uniform shape and size as they bake.) Bake for 5 minutes, rotate the pan front to back, and bake until the cookies look just barely set, about 5 minutes more. Transfer to a wire rack to cool, and serve warm or at room temperature.

Pairs well with *"Didn't It Rain"* by Mahalia Jackson

Almond Granita

Serves 8 to 10

1½ cups almond paste made
    with 50 percent sugar

4¼ cups whole milk

What I love about this granita is that it's refreshing on a hot day, but what's even more interesting is how incredibly fragrant it is, especially for a cold dessert. Be sure to use almond paste that contains only 50 percent sugar so it's not too sweet.

Scrape the almond paste into your blender.

In a small pan on high heat, bring the milk to a simmer. Pour the simmering milk over the almond paste and blend on low speed until the milk and paste are fully incorporated.

Pour the mixture into a shallow container and place in your freezer. Stir every 10 minutes with a fork to keep the solids from settling to the bottom before the liquid starts to freeze, about 1 hour. Cover the container and leave it in the freezer until the granita has turned to solid ice, at least 2 hours. Don't rush this step; the ice needs to be rock solid or the dish won't work.

About 10 minutes before serving, chill your serving glasses in the freezer.

Use a sturdy fork like a rake to scrape the ice into a pile at the bottom of the container. Scoop the ice into a chilled serving glass, then return the glass to the freezer as you prepare the other glasses (don't stress too much; it's still delicious if it's slightly melted). Serve immediately.

It helps to know: **This recipe requires a blender.**

Pairs well with "Everybody's Talkin'" by Iggy Pop

DRINKS, FOR ALWAYS

When my friends ask me what they should bring to my dinner party, my response goes one of two ways: vanilla ice cream or good wine. I have been enamored with the drink since I picked up a job in a wine shop at age seventeen. The legal age in New Orleans at the time was eighteen, so they'd let me stock the shelves and sneak into the tastings from time to time. Like cooking, wine lent itself well to my insatiable curiosity. Even more so, it satisfied my proclivity for romance.

Wine tells a story of place and personality. I became obsessed with the regionality of it, especially the wines from France. I love how each area is distinct: how the food and wine produced is specific to the location. They're almost always compatible—and this is no coincidence. I regard wine as food, as an integral part of the meal, and a vital part of the table.

It took me longer to learn to appreciate spirits. It wasn't until my mid-forties that I was finally mature enough to understand scotch, for example. Even so, it's the one beverage that I both respect and keep at a distance.

When choosing cocktails for this book, I focused on rhum agricole, the spirit that came into my life with ease. When I drink rhum, be it a Ti' Punch (page 271) after service, a Daiquiri (see page 272) on vacation, or a snifter of a dark, cask-aged spirit on my porch, I find myself on an island with the first sip: reading in a hammock, listening to live music, and smelling the salty ocean air.

When I'm not on vacation, I re-create that feeling on my days off at my home bar. At any given moment, it's destined to be stocked with cane syrup, 3 or 4 amaros, at least two gins, several bottles of light and dark rum, odds and ends of gifted whiskeys, bitters, vermouth, and a bottle of vodka in the freezer for the undiscerning.

Though I keep my shelves diverse, the Pink Palace is a haven for the rhum I like best. Originating in the French Caribbean, agricole blanc is made from sugarcane rather than molasses, which yields a massive difference in flavor and complexity. The French West Indies has mastered the spirit of the commoner. It can be on par with the world's best whiskeys.

You'll also find amaros, my favorite ingredient in a cocktail. I gravitate toward bitter liqueurs and drinks that aren't too sweet. Hence, the negroni (see page 268), a drink that would surely be included in the menu of my ultimate meal. There are a few outliers in this chapter as well: The margarita (see page 274), for example, mostly because it's Devin's favorite cocktail. I drink tequila in small, moderate doses, and I recommend that you do the same.

Every dinner party I host, no matter how casual, is a celebration. I start one of two ways: with champagne or a Ti' Punch. The true mascot of this book, the Ti' Punch demands respect. It's a sipper, unlike a margarita or a daiquiri, which you finish quickly and have another. The Ti' Punch forces you to slow down—that's part of what I love about it.

If you're attending a party at my house and you're one of the last to arrive, you'll find the group gathered around my kitchen island. I shuck oysters and serve drinks while my friends swap stories, gossip, and flirt, anticipating the meal to come. It's fun.

Many of these recipes can be prepared ahead of time, so you can spend more time socializing. Most are perfect to make just for yourself, maybe to enjoy on your porch at sunset. All are meant to allow you to revel in the conviviality of life.

Negroni, Three Ways

Serves 1

My "Classic"

1 large ice cube

1 ounce gin (I like Nolet's Silver)

1 ounce Campari

1 ounce Carpano Antica Formula
   sweet vermouth

Orange peel for garnish

The David

1 large ice cube

1½ ounces Charbay R5 hop-flavored
   whiskey

¾ ounce Carpano Antica Formula
   sweet vermouth

¾ ounce Aperol

½ ounce freshly squeezed Cara Cara
   orange juice

Cara Cara orange peel for garnish

Rhum Negroni

1 large ice cube

1 ounce Rhum J.M V.S.O.P. or
   barrel-aged rhum agricole

1 ounce Casoni 1814 Aperitivo

1 ounce Bonal Gentiane-Quina

Orange peel for garnish

The Ti' Punch (page 271) may be the mascot of this book, but if I had to pick one cocktail to drink for the rest of my life, it would be one of these negronis. They're bitter, classic, and taste best in summer, fall, winter, and spring.

Place a large ice cube in a rocks glass and pour the liquid ingredients over the top. Stir to combine. Rub the outside of the orange peel along the rim of the glass, then pinch it over the top of the glass to expel its oils. Garnish with the peel and serve (or drink!) immediately.

Pairs well with *"Prodigal Son" by The Rolling Stones*

➜ Clockwise from top: Rhum Negroni,
My "Classic", The David

Ti' Punch

Serves 2

1 lime
6 ounces rhum agricole
½ ounce cane syrup
2 large ice cubes

This is a true Tuesday-at-the-Pink-Palace kind of beverage: it's strong enough to only drink on my day off, and it has a way of making me feel like I'm on vacation, even on my "Sunday" night. I've made this drink according to how I've seen bartenders make it in the Caribbean, with one exception. On the islands, a Ti' Punch is served at room temperature, which is varsity-level when it comes to this cocktail. Drink that for a while, and you'll forget the name of your children. Unless I'm on vacation, I serve mine over a big ice cube and sip it slowly while the ice cube melts.

Set the lime on its side and slice off two opposite sides lengthwise, leaving about 1 inch of the lime's center left over. Cutting it this way prevents the larger cells in the center of the lime from getting into the drink, and I like the flavor of a more rind-heavy Ti' Punch.

Squeeze the two lime slices into a mixing glass. Add them to the glass and gently muddle the rind. Add the rhum and cane syrup and continue to muddle and mix until combined.

Put two large ice cubes into two serving glasses. Divide the punch between the two glasses, pouring it over the ice.

Slice a couple of small rind pieces from the remaining lime. Squeeze over the top of the drink, then add the rinds to the drink as a garnish. Serve.

Pairs well with *"Have Some Mercy" by Delroy Wilson*

Daiquiri

Serves 1

1 cup sugar

1½ ounces rhum agricole (preferred) or Plantation 3 Star rum (more traditional)

1 ounce freshly squeezed lime juice

Ice

1 lime round for garnish

A daiquiri has all of the elements I like in a cocktail: a clear spirit with a lot of citrus and acidity. A good daiquiri instantly brings me to my happy place, complete with plenty of sun and sea.

First, make a simple syrup by combining the sugar and 1 cup water in a small saucepan and bringing to a boil on high heat, stirring frequently, until the sugar dissolves. Let the syrup cool to room temperature before using. (Store any leftover syrup, covered, in your refrigerator for up to 3 weeks.)

To make the daiquiri, combine the rhum, 1 ounce simple syrup, and the lime juice in a cocktail shaker. Fill with ice and shake until very cold. Strain into a cocktail glass and garnish with a lime round floating on top. Serve.

Pairs well with *"Johnny Too Bad" by The Slickers*

A Blenderful of Frozen Daiquiris

Serves about 6

1 cup rhum agricole (preferred) or Plantation 3 Star rum (more traditional)

½ cup gum syrup

¾ cup freshly squeezed lime juice

6 cups ice

6 lime rounds for garnish

It helps to know: **This recipe (obviously) requires a blender.**

I would love to scoff at the frozen daiq (see photo at right), but they're too much fun to drink. For frozen cocktails, I use a rich syrup, preferably a gum arabic (I use one from Small Hand Foods), as it results in a better texture for the final cocktail.

In your blender, combine the rhum, syrup, lime juice, and ice. Blend on high speed until smooth. Divide among serving glasses and garnish with a lime. Serve.

Pairs well with *"Let's Call This" by Thelonious Monk*

Classic Margarita

Serves 1

Lime wedge

Salt or Tajín (for a kick) for a salted rim (optional)

Ice

1½ ounces tequila (I like reposado)

1 ounce Cointreau

1 ounce freshly squeezed lime juice

Honey (optional)

Though not a common indulgence for me personally, a margarita happens to be a favorite drink of Devin's and of my bar manager, Jason Strich; and as such it's included in this cookbook. This is the base recipe for a classic margarita, but it can be enjoyed in almost any combination of flavors to please any palate. Feel free to experiment with different citruses and make this recipe your own.

If you're salting the rim of your glass, rub the lime wedge around the perimeter of the glass, then spin the rim in the salt and shake off any excess. Fill the salted glass with ice and set aside.

Combine the tequila, Cointreau, and lime juice in a cocktail shaker. If you prefer a sweeter drink, add honey to taste. Add ice and shake until cold, then strain into your ice-filled glass. Garnish with the lime wedge and serve.

Pairs well with *"Zombie" by Fela Kuti*

Mezcal Margarita

Serves 1

Lime wedge

Salt for a salted rim (optional)

Ice

1 ounce tequila (I like reposado)

½ ounce mezcal

1 ounce Cointreau

1 ounce freshly squeezed lime juice

Honey (optional)

A smooth margarita with a subtle, smoky surprise—why not?

If you're salting the rim of your glass, rub the lime wedge around the perimeter of the glass, then spin the rim in the salt and shake off any excess. Fill the salted glass with ice and set aside.

Combine the tequila, mezcal, Cointreau, and lime juice in a cocktail shaker. If you prefer a sweeter drink, add honey to taste. Add ice and shake until cold, then strain into your ice-filled glass. Garnish with the lime wedge and serve.

Pairs well with *"How Can I Lose" by Shirley Ann Lee*

Sangria, Two Ways

Serves 6 to 8

Sangria is your chance to be creative with whatever fruit is in season. I really love to use stone fruits like peaches and nectarines, but berries or even ripe persimmons also work nicely. These two sangrias are meant to serve six to eight people, but they go down easy and fast. You may want to consider doubling the recipe if you have room in your refrigerator.

Simple Sangria

1 (750-ml) bottle dry rosé wine

1 cup gin (I prefer Nolet's Silver)

1 cup Aperol

½ cup orange blossom honey

2 lemons, sliced

1 orange, sliced

2 grapefruits, sliced

1 apple, cored and sliced

1 pear, cored and sliced

Soda water

Fresh mint for garnish

Edible flowers for garnish (optional)

It helps to know: **This sangria sits overnight.**

Pour the rosé, gin, Aperol, and honey in a large sealable container and stir to combine. Add the fruit and let it rest overnight in your refrigerator.

To serve, ladle the sangria into wineglasses and top with a splash of soda water. Garnish with the mint, edible flowers, and a few pieces of the macerated fruit.

continued

Pink Palace Sangria

¾ cup lemon peels (from about
   5 lemons)

1½ cups sugar

1½ cups freshly squeezed lemon juice

1 (750-ml) bottle dry rosé wine

1¼ cups freshly squeezed
   grapefruit juice

½ cup pisco

½ cup raspberries or strawberries,
   or a mix of both

Soda water

To make a lemon cordial, combine the lemon peels and sugar in a small container. Cover and shake lightly to mix. Let sit at room temperature overnight. The next day, add the lemon juice and stir to dissolve the sugar. Strain over a jar, discard the peels, cover, and refrigerate the cordial. You should have about 1¼ cups. (Store any leftover cordial, covered, in your refrigerator for up to 1 month.)

To make the sangria, combine ¾ cup of the lemon cordial, the rosé, grapefruit juice, pisco, and berries in a large pitcher and stir to combine. Cover and refrigerate (ideally overnight) until you are ready to serve.

To serve, ladle the sangria into wine glasses and top with a splash of soda water. Garnish with a few macerated berries per glass.

Pairs well with "Los Dos" by Los Panchos

Ginger Beer Classics with Fresh Syrup, Three Ways

Serves 1

I use ginger beer for effortlessly entertaining at home because I can make a wide variety of cocktails from it with very little effort. A seasonal twist can be added with nothing more than your favorite fruits and vegetables, some sugar, and a pinch of salt. The salt and sugar draw out the moisture from the fruit, leaving a fresh syrup for flavor and leftover fruit for garnish. (Without the syrup, these are the classic cocktails we all know and love.) These recipes make enough syrup for 8 to 10 cocktails, and any leftovers can be stored, covered, in your refrigerator for up to 5 days.

Moscow Mule with Fresh Strawberry Syrup

2 cups washed, hulled (see page 71), and thinly sliced strawberries

½ cup sugar

Salt

Ice

1½ ounces vodka, or spirit of your choice

½ ounce freshly squeezed lime juice

4 ounces ginger beer (I like Fever-Tree)

1 lime round for garnish

In a bowl, toss together the strawberries, sugar, and a pinch of salt. Cover and let sit in a warm place for 2 hours. Strain the syrup over a bowl, reserving both the liquid and the strawberry slices.

Fill a serving glass (a copper mug is traditional but not necessary) with ice. Pour in the vodka, lime juice, ginger beer, and ½ ounce of the fresh strawberry syrup. Stir to combine. Garnish with a lime round and, if you like, a couple of strawberry slices. Serve.

Dark & Stormy with Fresh Blackberry Syrup

1 cup blackberries

¼ cup sugar

Salt

Ice

½ ounce freshly squeezed lime juice

4 ounces ginger beer (I like Fever-Tree)

2 ounces rum (I like Gosling's Black Seal)

1 lime round for garnish

In a bowl, toss together the blackberries, sugar, and a pinch of salt. Cover and let sit in a warm place for 2 hours. Strain the syrup over a bowl, reserving both the liquid and the berries.

Fill a tall glass with ice. Add the lime juice, ginger beer, and ½ ounce of the fresh blackberry syrup and stir to combine. Slowly pour in the rum so it floats on top of the ginger beer. Garnish with a lime round and a small spoonful of the berries. Serve.

continued

El Diablo with Fresh Beet Syrup

1 large beet

¼ cup sugar

Salt

Ice

1½ ounces tequila (I like reposado)

¼ to ½ ounce crème de cassis

½ ounce freshly squeezed lime juice

4 ounces ginger beer (I like Fever-Tree)

1 lime round for garnish

Peel and thinly slice the beet using a mandoline or box grater. In a bowl, toss the beet slices with the sugar and a pinch of salt. Cover and let sit in a warm place for 2 hours. Strain over a bowl, discarding the solids and reserving the rich and earthy beet syrup.

Fill a tall glass with ice. Add the tequila, crème de cassis, lime juice, ginger beer, and ½ ounce of the beet syrup and stir to combine. Garnish with a lime round. Serve.

Pairs well with "She's the One That's Got It" by Tav Falco and Panther Burns

⇢ Clockwise from top: Moscow Mule, El Diablo with Fresh Beet Syrup, Dark & Stormy with Fresh Blackberry Syrup

A (Humble) How-To on Buying Wine

I could probably count on just one hand the number of times I've brought a bottle of wine to a restaurant. Though I must've brought my own bottle at some point, I can't even think of a time in recent memory when I've walked up to a restaurant with a bottle that wasn't a gift for the kitchen. My best bottles, wines I've saved and anticipated for months, glasses that become some of my most cherished memories, are always opened in my home.

Though I love going out for a glass of wine just as much as the average person, I enjoy bottles at home in a way that I never could in a restaurant. I'll hoard a bottle for just the right occasion, letting a magnum of champagne collect dust in my cabinet for a full year in anticipation of a party, an anniversary, a birthday, or a friend visiting from out of town. To me, a truly special bottle of wine at home can be an emotional experience. When I finally open it and I'm drinking a glass surrounded by my loved ones, it's worth every square inch of shelf space it occupied and more.

I believe a significant part of the enjoyment of wine is a product of place. I was traveling in France many years ago and fell in love with a white wine from a small producer that I couldn't find in the United States. I liked it so much that I had a case shipped home. I couldn't wait for it to arrive, but when I tasted it in California, it didn't even taste like the same wine. That was a lesson learned. To me, the enjoyment of wine comes down to my surroundings, my mindset, and the people I'm with. Wine often doesn't hold its value when it's taken out of context. I'm not being critical; quite the opposite. That's something I love about wine—its uncanny ability to reveal a sense of place.

For a special bottle, I look for wines that are profound—that exhibit their sense of place with force. They transcend the need to drink them where they're produced or in exactly the perfect context. Less vivid in my memory, though just as special in a different way, are all of the bottles that I open on an average Tuesday night, unwinding by myself or with a couple of close friends. Wines that are enjoyable but perhaps not profound are perfectly acceptable on a Tuesday. What's more, staying at home is my opportunity to create a sense of place of my own.

When it comes to selecting wine to drink at home, my philosophy is simple: I buy tried-and-true favorites and I taste new things with an open mind. Following are some personal preferences I've developed over the years, but take them as my opinion rather than fact. To me, wine is food, and, like food, it's meant to be fun. I encourage you to spend time finding the bottles that are uniquely special to you.

I like to drink red wines in the fall and winter, light and dancing white wines in the spring and summer, and rosé year-round. I like California wines if they're balanced and not overly clean. I don't want to say I like dirty wine, but I do like wine with character, with a little grit and earth that tells a story. I don't like wines made with precision, with the perfect acidity and alcohol levels. They're good on paper but have no personality: they're clinical in my opinion.

I have a certain affinity for French wines because I've spent so much time there, both personally and professionally. I like wines that are well balanced because they go best with food without dominating. I also like wines that tell you where they're from: like a Nebbiolo from Piedmont or a Burgundy from France or a Pinot Noir from the Santa Cruz mountains. This preference also applies to blends. Bordeaux, for example, is very rarely from one grape, but it's blended in a style that represents not only the producer but also the region.

I love the wines, both red and white, from the Loire Valley because they tend to have both fantastic value and quality. I like rosé because it's so versatile: you can drink it with both traditionally red or white wine dishes. I like Riesling in general, but especially Riesling from Germany. And, of course, I love champagne, but who doesn't? Like the saying goes, "It's like drinking stars."

I don't want to be too specific because I strongly believe you should find the bottles that bring you joy. If you truly don't know where to start and don't have a wine store nearby with a friendly and patient person to help you, try focusing on a reputable importer. I've long been a fan of Kermit Lynch, but if you find a wine that you like, try other wines from the same importer. The importer can often be a reliable resource, almost like having your own sommelier hand-selecting wines for you to experiment with at home.

Your home is where you get to create your own sense of place, but it's also where you can experiment and try new things—and maybe even fail. What's most important is that you keep an open mind. If you try something new and it doesn't completely work out, you've still learned something that can be used as a reference point in the future. Remember, in the end, it's just dinner, and it's just a bottle of wine.

A Green Juice

Serves 2

4 heaping tablespoons plain yogurt

4 ribs celery, cut into 1-inch pieces

1 cucumber, peeled, ends trimmed,
    and cut into 1-inch slices

2 Granny Smith apples, cored and
    quartered

½-inch piece fresh ginger, peeled

Large handful of spinach leaves, long
    tough stems discarded

12 mint leaves

It helps to know: **This recipe
requires a blender.**

Green juice is easily nutritious, but making it tasty can be a
challenge. I find that the sweetness of apple and freshness of
mint make this green juice one you'll actually enjoy. I drink it
for a healthy start to my morning during the month preceding
Mardi Gras, when I abstain from the other drinks in this chapter
(excluding coffee of course) or just to have some balance during
the rest of the year. Feel free to use your juicer if you have one,
but I prefer to use a blender to keep the fruits' and vegetables'
natural fiber.

Combine the yogurt, celery, cucumber, apples, ginger, and ½ cup water
in a blender and pulse until pureed. Add the spinach and mint leaves and
pulse until incorporated. Serve.

Pairs well with "69 Année Érotique" by Serge Gainsbourg and Jane Birkin

A Nice Cup of Coffee

20 grams coffee
About 350 grams boiling water

Most mornings I wake up, put on a record, and make myself a cup of coffee. I grind my beans by hand—a morning ritual I thoroughly enjoy despite sometimes enduring some snide comments from friends. Whether you grind your coffee the old-fashioned way or not, I recommend investing in a high-quality grinder as the coffee will extract differently depending on the size of the grounds. And, as I've said before and I'll say again, a scale is one of the greatest kitchen tools you can buy for under $15.

Grind the coffee for a paper filter; it should look about the size of a fine sand. Set the paper filter in your brewing device over your mug. Pour boiling water over the filter, heating your mug and rinsing off any papery taste from the filter. Discard the water.

Spoon the coffee into the filter, shaking to level the grounds. Tare your scale so it reads 0. Start a timer and slowly pour around 50 grams of boiling water into the center of the coffee, being careful not to touch the sides of the filter. Wait 30 to 45 seconds as the coffee rises and bubbles, releasing its carbon dioxide.

Slowly pour boiling water in a circular motion starting in the center and moving outward until the filter is three-quarters full, still being careful not to touch the side of the filter (or the water will go straight through to the cup). Wait as the water drips through the coffee into your mug, and a darker crust forms around the perimeter of the grounds.

It helps to know: This recipe requires a scale, a brewing device (such as a V60 or small dripper; I use a Kalita Wave), and a paper filter. Though not necessary, a spouted kettle also helps with accuracy.

Continue with this process until you've added about 300 grams of boiling water and the timer reads between 3 and 4 minutes. (If it takes more time, your grind is likely too fine. If it takes less time, your grind is likely too coarse). Serve.

Pairs well with *"Teenage Kicks" by The Undertones*

Acknowledgments

This project was a team effort that wouldn't have been possible without the help of my friends, family, and so many invaluable members of the Manresa universe. I am forever grateful for all of your daily support, and particularly in the creation of this cookbook.

A very special thank you goes out to all the patrons of the Pink Palace parties, especially Maisie Ganzler (for letting us borrow your gorgeous home and so much more), Can Ağaoğlu (for being Devin's favorite plus-one and so much more), Katy Oursler, Stephen Beaumier, Chef Stephanie Prida, our dear Nic Kapellas, Tricia Mitchell, Liz Birnbaum, Chef Jeffrey Wall, Chef Nicholas Romero, Christopher Harris, and Jenny "Chef Jen" Yun. My home wouldn't be such a warm and lively place without your frequent visits, and this book couldn't have been made without all the memories.

To the team at Mentone Restaurant, led by Chef Matthew Bowden and Chris Sullivan, for graciously sharing your space for our final photo shoot. To the staff at The Bywater, for supplying our first meetings with warm hospitality and many, many oysters. To Daniel D'Amico and Ava Sonleitner, members of our Manresa team with undoubtedly bright futures, for kindly helping me prepare, organize, and style dishes for the photos in this book.

To Avery Ruzicka, my partner at Manresa Bread, for providing my favorite cookie and grilled cheese recipes. To Jason Strich, the Bar Director for all things Manresa, for helping me develop many of the cocktail recipes in this book. To Courtney Weyl, the Pastry Chef at Manresa, for helping me with all things sweet.

To Jim Rollston, Manresa's Wine Director, and my friend John Locke for supplying many of my dinner parties with your own special bottles.

Devin and I would also like to thank everyone who helped test recipes in their own home kitchens, especially Mike Chack, Sydney Mimeles, Leah Pettus, and Shirley Fuller. Thomas Pettus-Czar, thank you for your edits between chess moves.

Aya Brackett, you have impressed me greatly with your talent, patience, and willingness to go full speed with me for a few hectic days at a time. Much appreciation goes to Glenn Jenkins, for trusting us with your collection, and to Summer Wilson for your photo assistance. Finally, a big thank you to Julie Bennett for your thoughtful edits, Emma Campion for your art direction, and the entire team at Ten Speed Press for believing in this project.

Thank you to all the patrons of the Pink Palace

Index

Published in the United States by Ten Speed Press, an imprint of Random House,
a division of Penguin Random House LLC, New York.
www.tenspeed.com

Ten Speed Press and the Ten Speed Press colophon are registered
trademarks of Penguin Random House LLC.

Library of Congress Control Number: 2020944752.

Hardcover ISBN: 978-1-9848-5850-4
eBook ISBN: 978-1-9848-5851-1

Printed in China

Editor: Julie Bennett
Designer & art director: Emma Campion
Production designers: Mari Gill and Andi Watstein
Production manager: Serena Sigona
Prepress color manager: Jane Chinn
Typeface designer: Ashleigh Brewer (Mentone Block)
Food stylist: David Kinch | Prop stylist: Glenn Jenkins
Photo assistant: Summer Wilson
Copyeditor: Andrea Chesman | Proofreader: Linda Bouchard
Indexer: Ken DellaPenta
Marketer: Allison Renzulli | Publicist: Kristin Casemore

10 9 8 7 6 5 4 3 2 1

First Edition